crazy
faith

crazy faith

ordinary people, extraordinary lives

SUSAN K. WILLIAMS SMITH

JUDSON PRESS
PUBLISHERS SINCE 1824
VALLEY FORGE, PA

crazy faith: ordinary people, extraordinary lives

Judson Press and the author have made every effort to trace the ownership of all quotes. In the event of a question arising from the use of a quote, we regret any error made and will be pleased to make the necessary correction in future printings and editions of this book.

Bible quotations in this volume are from *The Holy Bible*, King James Version (KJV); from the New Revised Standard Version (NRSV), copyright © 1989 by the Division of Christian Education of the National Council of the Churches of Christ in the United States of America, used by permission; all rights reserved; and from THE MESSAGE, copyright © 1993, 1994, 1995, used by permission of NavPress Publishing Group.

Library of Congress Cataloging-in-Publication Data
Smith, Susan K. Williams, 1954-
Crazy faith : ordinary people, extraordinary lives / Susan Smith.
p. cm.
ISBN 978-0-8170-1531-2 (pbk. : alk. paper) 1. Faith. 2. Spirituality. I. Title.
BV4637.S5575 2008
234'.23—dc22
2008005899

Printed in the U.S.A.
First Edition, 2009.

To my two children, Caroline and Charlie,
who have taught me that
it takes crazy faith
to make it in a crazy world

And to everyone who
has ever wondered
if having faith
is all it is
pumped up
to be

CONTENTS

Foreword   …ix

Acknowledgments   …x

Preface   …xii

Introduction   …xviii

1: Why Faith?   …1

2: Before I Be a Slave   …9

3: God's Ridiculous Expectations   …20

4: Roses and a Key   …28

5: You're Not the Boss of Me!   …37

6: Waiting for Deliverance   …47

7: Questions, Trumpets, and Jars   …55

8: Where to Go, Not How to Get There   …65

9: The Most Audacious Touch   …75

10: The Eighth Wonder of the World   …84

11: How Shall They Eat?   …94

12: The Scales Fell from My Eyes   …102

Conclusion: The Miracles around Us   …112

Notes   …121

foreword

Susan Smith has given us a mighty work that retells the stories of those who have turned vision, faith, and action into marvels of human accomplishment. *Crazy Faith: Ordinary People, Extraordinary Lives* reminds us that faith is not a destination, but a journey, and along the way, each of us can become an instrument of God's miracles. In the stories of the s/heroes with whom we journey in the book, we discover, affirm, and renew the seeds of the crazy faith that lie within each of us.

Crazy Faith celebrates the uniqueness and diversity of God's people to be instruments of God's will on earth. It is a compelling read for many different audiences, from Bible study classes to social book clubs, from seasoned saints to new converts. The mystery and power of God are revealed in the lives and accomplishments of persons such as Mary McLeod Bethune, Nelson Mandela, Mother Teresa, Emily Washington, and Chris Gardner. Their stories, paralleled by references to sacred texts, teach us that difficult circumstances and hard questions about God can fuel the faith of ordinary people to make extraordinary things happen. In this time of new possibilities for transformative change in the world, *Crazy Faith* is a must-read for the new generation, so that adolescents and young adults might capture the spirit of belief in the unseeable and impossible to make the world a better place. *Crazy Faith* is indeed a book for such a time as this!

Dr. Iva E. Carruthers, Secretary General
Samuel DeWitt Proctor Conference

acknowledgments

I think that every book I write will forever be dedicated to my deceased mother, Mary Lee Simmons, and my children, Caroline and Charlie. Those three individuals have made the most profound impact on my life, and without them and the experiences that we have had and continue to have, I would not write at all.

But with each book there are different people who play a specifically unique role, and for this book that reality is no different. I have to acknowledge these very special people who helped, prayed, edited, discussed, criticized, and just listened to me as this book was being written.

First, I thank Diane Williams and Dr. Cynthia Tyson, to whom I sent every single chapter as it was written. I don't know what work of their own they interrupted to read my work, but they did so and never complained; in fact, they seemed eager to read, which made me eager to write more.

I thank my sister-friends who helped me make copies, type endnotes, and do all that the editor requires when I was ready to send the manuscript to the publisher. Rev. Patricia Battle, Dr. Cynthia Tyson, Dr. Judy Alston, Diane Williams, and Jennifer Davis stayed with me late into the evening doing what we had to do. We made it a party. It was a special time for me, and I want them to know it.

Rebecca Irwin-Diehl, editor at Judson Press, I give you my thanks for acting on crazy faith and reading my proposal, which is now this book. I so appreciate you and Judson.

I thank my pastor, Rev. Dr. Jeremiah A. Wright Jr., who, in spite of how the media has portrayed him, is singularly the most brilliant, most spiritual, most compassionate pastor I have ever met or known. I thank you, Pastor Wright, because no matter what you've gone through, in all the years we've been friends, you have always "been there" for your flock, me included. For that I am so grateful. That is an amazing accomplishment and a trait that I have tried to emulate as a pastor. I don't come close, so I have to be content with the honor of having been one of your students.

I thank my sister-friend Dr. Iva Carruthers, who has the most amazing faith and vision that I have ever seen. I think of you, Dr. Iva, in the same way I think of Mary McLeod Bethune and Harriet Tubman. Your work with the Samuel DeWitt Proctor Conference is changing the world. You move forward with nothing but faith, and God rewards your work. You truly are a role model.

Then, finally, I thank my editor, Rhoda McKinney-Jones. Rho, you are the best editor ever. No writer is worth anything without a good editor, one who knows and understands the writer's heart, spirit, and intent. I was amazed and humbled that in spite of your beloved father being critically ill, you took my manuscript across the country with you and edited as you worried about him. My prayer is that something within these pages helped you through that very difficult time. I cannot thank you enough. I love you.

Finally, I acknowledge the God I love, the God that Dr. Judy Alston says "has jokes." I think that Sarah, Moses, Gideon, David, and Noah probably thought the same thing.

That's why to believe in God takes crazy faith.

I love you all.

preface

Not long ago, my sister was stricken with an illness. Doctors said that she had a thyroid condition and began treating her. But after some time, it became clear that something was terribly wrong. In spite of taking her medicine, she was getting worse, and one day she lost consciousness while she was at home. She was rushed to the hospital, where it was found that instead of having a thyroid condition, she had Hodgkin's disease. She was critically ill, and she remained in intensive care for what seemed like months, sustained by machines and medicines.

I thought that her time on earth had passed, but then, out of nowhere, she rallied and got better. I don't mean a little better, but completely. It was a miracle in my eyes. Some time later, after she had fully recovered and we were talking, I asked her, "Did you ever think you were going to die?" And without flinching, pausing, or blinking, she said, "No."

Her answer was so final and so resolute that it made me wonder what her journey had been like, from being critically ill to being well. I didn't ask. But I do remember thinking that she had some kind of faith, a faith that I didn't know if I would have had, had I been in her shoes.

Since then, I have wondered about faith—what it is and isn't, who has it and who doesn't and why. I have walked with eyes and ears wide open, looking for a way to see faith, taste it, and explain it. Religion and its handling and discussions of faith actually scared me. It seemed, as I listened to preachers talk about it and recount biblical stories, that faith was something possessed only by extraordinarily religious people. I would never have done what Abraham and Sarah did, believing God for a child past menopause and potency. I wasn't sure that I could be like Rahab, believing that foreign invaders would prove to be trustworthy in saving me from destruction. I knew I would have balked if God ever told me to do something as crazy as building a huge ark in preparation for a flood when a single raindrop hadn't fallen. Though I loved, and still love, the biblical stories, the faith of those saints seemed unattainable to me. They were our inspiration and our role models, but I couldn't hope to achieve their level of spiritual accomplishments. That's why they were in the Bible, I decided. It made for good reading, but it wasn't a realistic way to try to live my own ordinary life.

But as I have watched people, and listened to people, and seen what people have done *on faith*, my mind has changed. It's not necessarily extraordinary people who have changed the world, but rather ordinary people who have been willing to act and live on faith. The world has been shaped and changed by people who literally see the impossible, or at least believe they can. Great things have been done by plain, everyday people. With faith, which really is vision fueled by action, I have seen people blossom into new life as they make the impossible become possible.

A friend of mine decided that God was leading her to start a school. She had no experience in education; her degree was in history. But she could *see* this school. I wouldn't have known what to do first, and neither did she. The only thing that she had was this feeling that God was in it, and she said that if God had told her to do the school, then God would show her how. I watched in awe as the pieces of this giant project began to fall into place. It was like she didn't have to do anything except continue to believe that the school was possible, in spite of her lack of credentials and experience. The result was a first-class school, teaching children grades one through eight, a school so excellent that it has won awards in education.

It was a vision fueled by action, enabling her to do the impossible. It occurred to me that this special kind of vision comes to different people in different ways. Another friend saw an old, run-down house and got excited. I looked at the same house and saw nothing. In fact, I was inclined to say that it should be torn down. It was a mess, infested with rodents and bugs. But he could *see* this house redone. And true to his vision, he transformed the house into a showpiece. I could see nothing, but he could.

I continued to watch people and to think about what they were doing in comparison to what the biblical characters I loved so much had done. I knew that these people weren't special. They simply had an ability to see something that wasn't there, and they had an ability to believe that God was in their lives and in what they saw. When I thought about the biblical stories, it occurred to me that these people were not much different. They weren't priests or socialites or mayors or anything special. They were just people who dared to act on what they saw and heard. They were not dissuaded or discouraged by naysayers or by the difficulty in doing what they could see.

So faith, crazy faith, is the ability to make the invisible visible and the impossible possible. My friends had it, and the biblical characters had it. What they saw or believed wasn't practical or logical. There was no reason to believe that what they saw could or would happen, and yet they believed it anyway. Crazy faith—believing in the impossible when everyone else says, "That's crazy."

Was what these people had simply a lot of confidence? What was the difference between having crazy faith and having confidence? People who are not religious have been able to do the impossible too. Donald Trump doesn't strike me as a religious person, yet he sees things that nobody else sees. The common denominator between faith and confidence is this ability to see and to have one's vision fueled by action. But faith is all the more remarkable because there is no logic to believing what one believes. At least Trump relies on tried and tested financial and business principles that, if followed, are likely to yield success.

But with faith, the only staple involved is God, an entity who is by no means logical or practical. There is no neat formula that, if added up correctly, will yield a specific product. There is only this invisible spirit, with a voice that sometimes is heard by nobody except the one with the crazy vision. In *The American Heritage Dictionary of the English Language*, faith is defined as "a confident belief in the truth, value, or worthiness of a person, idea, or thing; belief that does not rest on logical proof or material evidence." A person who is confident, by contrast, has "assurance or certainty."

What the stories of Scripture and of the visionary people around me reveal is that in order to have crazy faith, one must be willing and able to submit completely to the possibility of God being God. Take Mary the mother of Jesus, for example. She became a single mother after an angel appeared and told her that she would give birth to the Son of God. And then, was she supposed to tell the man to whom she was engaged that she was pregnant, and honestly believe that he would not abandon her? That's some major crazy faith. So Mary's response to the angel, "I am the Lord's servant. May it be to me as you have said" (Luke 1:38), strikes me as being crucial for having crazy faith and as typically being present in those people in the Bible and in contemporary life who have it.

The only "sure thing" that one has in hearing a command from God or seeing something that seems absolutely impossible is God, and if one is to live a life of faith, one has to believe that God truly can do the impossible. There is a willing submission of spirit and will that must take place; that submission seems to open up a conduit between God and the child of God that allows God's power to move through, and produce extraordinary things through, ordinary people.

The Bible is filled with stories of God saying, in one way or another, "Try me." And when people let go of their natural tendency to doubt or to fall into despair, faith is fueled by action, and God does amazing things. We, the people, don't do the things that God proposes. It's the God in us who does them. We are merely the vessels.

Perhaps most comforting of all the lessons contained in the Bible is that God uses imperfect people to do divine work. David was an unimpressive shepherd with an eye for women. Abraham was a passive husband and father who endangered his wife and sons to avoid conflict. Moses had a speech impediment and a hot temper. Rahab was a prostitute. Nowhere does it say or indicate in the Bible that God is looking for outstanding individuals. But what God does want, or what seems to be necessary for the inexplicable power of God to be revealed through human beings, is an ability and desire to submit totally to God in order to be extraordinarily empowered.

The skeptic will scoff at this. This is really religious talk. And the skeptic will ask why we need God when any person who has a good amount of confidence can do great things. Here's the difference: In the world, imperfection cancels out confidence. One mistake can often, depending on our self-confidence and their factors, disqualify us from any chance of future success. In God's reign, no one has to be perfect. We can come to God with nothing but a hunger to be close to God. God doesn't hold our humanity against us. We just have to be willing to believe that God can and will help us overcome our weaknesses, or better yet, use our weaknesses on God's behalf. And the more God does in us and through us, the more the divine vision is fueled by action; the more this fueled action becomes a part of our lives, the more the glory of God shines through.

And so in this book we will look at some people with crazy faith, messed-up people who were deemed worthy by God to get the word out that God is God.

This book is simply about believing and having extraordinary faith during challenging times—crazy faith. So we will look at Moses and Gideon and David, and the widow who was guided out of debt by Elisha, and the woman who was healed when she touched Jesus' garment. We will look at Mother Teresa and Nelson Mandela. We will look at Jesus' disciples and the people who sat on a hill and saw the feeding of the five thousand take place before their very eyes. We will look at Harriet Tubman, who dared to believe that a former slave could lead other slaves to freedom. We will look at Washington Roebling, who directed the building of the Brooklyn Bridge from his sickbed. We will look at Mary McLeod Bethune, who, in spite of racism and sexism, had faith crazy enough to make her believe that she could build a college.

Surely, crazy faith has shaped our world. Crazy faith, ordinary people, extraordinary lives.

introduction
faith versus crazy faith

We are a visual people. That is no new thing. When Jesus was on earth, most of the disciples believed that he had risen from the dead and had visited them, but there was one, Thomas, who did not believe. He said, "Unless I see the nail marks in his hands and put my finger where the nails were, … I will not believe it" (John 20:25). From our pews and places of self-righteousness, we condemn Thomas and wonder how he could have been so doubtful.

But if the truth be told, we're one only step away from, if not actually in sync with, Thomas. We have a need *to see* before we believe. We need concrete proof, and we are very reluctant, for the most part, to give credence to the idea that there are miracles that come from God. When something phenomenal occurs, we often are at a loss for words and try our best to "explain" what cannot be explained. We usually only half-heartedly admit that maybe this event came from God. More often than not, we simply say that what occurred was amazing and a miracle just happened.

To have faith, in the religious sense, requires a certain type of relationship with God. This is something that most of us do not have. When I asked a young woman in my congregation if she had faith, she said that she thought so, but wasn't sure. When I asked her why, she said, "Because if having faith means doing what God wants me to do, I don't have it, because I want to do what I want to do." Her statement probably resonates with most of us.

Having faith is the core of any religious system, but many religious people don't have it. The reason is because faith is a gift. Just as some people have the ability to teach, others to preach, others to dance, and some to sing, *to be able* to believe, against all odds, in what you cannot see is a gift. The good news is that this gift is ours for the asking (Matthew 7:7). This doesn't mean that we don't have to work to cultivate the gift of faith. After all, we've already established that faith at its core is vision fueled by *action*.

Faith in something higher than one's self produces its own humility. A person who has faith can do great things but gives credit to someone or something other than and higher than the self. That's why I say that there can be no real faith until there is a real relationship with God. One has to talk with God and walk with God daily. One has to develop ears that hear and eyes that see—eyes that *look for* God in all things. A person's heart must be trimmed of the calluses that life causes in order to make room for a God who loves and cares for all of God's children.

When that happens, one begins to hear God, and the more one hears God, the deeper one's faith grows. One of my favorite stories is that of Peter Marshall, born and raised in Scotland, who was the chaplain of the United States Senate in the late 1940s. He wrote in one of his books about how he was wrestling with God over his call to ministry as he was walking alone on a very dark and cloudy Scottish night. He heard a voice say, "Stop," but he kept going. He heard the voice again, and again he kept going. But when he heard it the third time, he stopped and stretched out on the ground where he was. He fell asleep. When he awoke, it was morning, and to his amazement, he was at the edge of a cliff. Had he taken another step, he would have fallen to his death. His ability to hear the voice of God had saved his life. No doubt it increased his faith as well!

Part of the relationship-building process that we enjoy with God brings things into perspective. We recognize who God is and what

God does. We learn that there is a vastness to God that we will strive our whole lives to learn and appreciate. And the more we come to know God, the more we learn to trust. That's another synonym for faith, and it's a key facet of our relationship with God. No relationship can thrive without trust.

If we take the time to build a relationship with God, we will begin to see God in everything and begin to nurture a seed of certainty that with God, all things are possible. If we don't build that relationship, we are handicapped in our religious walks by our natural tendency to take all that God has done for granted and to not believe something unless we see it with our own eyes.

A lack of trust hampers God from being God in our lives, and therefore it hampers the full development of our faith.

Don't misunderstand. Faith doesn't require us only to "be still and know" that God is God. Eventually that knowledge of God inspires action. Faith demands movement. It demands movement from the jowls of human limitation into the arms of divine expectation. Faith demands that the scales of inadequate human eyesight fall off to reveal new eyes, eyes that are, in essence, the very eyes of God. Faith demands the struggle to get loose from oneself and run into the arms of God, ready to be moved and directed into the place where God always intended us to be. And most important, faith demands that we move from *thinking* God can to *knowing* God can. To know is to "be certain beyond doubt." What one knows cannot be shaken. What one believes, however, can be influenced by a variety of factors. Faith is *knowing* what one knows—in this case, that God is and God can. Faith also is knowing that *you can* because of something or someone greater than you, no matter how impossible or senseless the situation that you are facing seems to be.

God wants us to try faith and get the taste of divine intervention in our lives. God wants us to try living out our faith, pushing fear aside, because fear cancels out faith. God wants us to see how amazing God really is. And because God is "in it," it will be.

So what is faith? Mere faith is simply the comfort of knowing that God is out there. We don't really put anything into developing this kind of faith. We're just glad that there is a God, and we know this because our parents or our pastor or someone else has told us, and we believe it.

Real faith comes as a result of our growing up and wanting a deeper spiritual life. We might have been told what is good, but we have to "test the waters" and look for God ourselves. Then we begin to question God—who God is and what God does, and why. And while developing our real faith, we will face some of the most serious faith crises. We wrestle with God because somehow, in the mere-faith stage, we think that God is simply "good," meaning that bad things won't happen to people who believe. We look at the condition of the world—widespread starvation, disease, and war—and we're confused. Who is this God? Is God really omnipotent? If God is good, why do bad things happen to good people? That was the question that Rabbi Harold Kushner posed in 1981 in his book *When Bad Things Happen to Good People*. It is during this stage of our faith development that many of us turn away from God because we don't understand. We don't appreciate or understand what we see. We grow angry because our understanding, in the mere-faith stage of our lives, was that faith in God was supposed to give us an easy time. When we see that this isn't true, we become disenchanted. We don't reject God altogether, for there is enough faith to tide us over. But we don't embrace God fully either, nor do we trust him completely. We're not about to say, as Mary did, "May it be to me as you have said" (in the King James Version the verse has even more punch: "Be it done unto me according to thy will"). We can't say that even while we're in the real-faith phase of our spiritual growth, at least not for a while. When we have mere faith, we are babes in the Lord. In the real-faith stage, we have become spiritual adolescents, with all the questions, behaviors, and rebellion that come with that phase of life. We have to go through it in order to get to crazy faith.

When we get to crazy faith, we still have dark moments, and things still go wrong. We still have periods when we doubt, but we are willing to let God have God's way in our lives. The biggest thing is that we now trust God like Mary did. Since we trust God's voice and vision, we now trust God's intentions for our lives. We know that bad things will happen in spite of our deep faith, but that knowledge will not throw us off course. Everything we do is God-driven in this phase of our lives. We get the "eyes to see and ears to hear" that Jesus mentions in the Gospels, and that makes a difference in how we view life and live life.

So, if that is faith, what is *crazy faith*?

That's simple. Crazy faith is knowing that God can and will do the most incredible things in the most impossible of situations. *Crazy faith.*

Composers and musicians throughout the ages have written about the importance of crazy faith. In his hymn text "Amazing Grace" John Newton wrote, "The Lord has promised good to me / His word my hope secures / He will my shield and portion be / As long as life endures." And Joe Darion wrote the lyrics to "The Impossible Dream," which proclaims the struggle of one man who fought "for the right, without question or pause, to be willing to march into hell for a heavenly cause." That is major crazy faith!

Having crazy faith requires a dogged determination to believe beyond all doubts, to be able to see the end in sight, and to trust God totally. Faith in God doesn't mean that the result will come without problems, issues, and probably some pain. Having crazy faith means that one knows all that and still believes.

Having crazy faith is a decision. It means that one decides to take God for who God is. People with crazy faith believe that God hears them and they hear God, and that God loves them enough to sustain them. People with crazy faith believe the visions that God gives them, and they know that since God gave the vision, God will supply the provision, no matter how long it takes. People with crazy faith thank God for that vision, no matter how ridiculous it seems. People with crazy faith know that God has seen something special in them.

People with crazy faith have a contagious spirit, strong enough to gather other people into the vision and strong enough to fend off people who would get in God's way. People with crazy faith know that the world and its work belong to God and understand that they are vessels of that vision. People with crazy faith know that God can do anything. They see mountains and either climb them or move them. They hear problems and pray through them, around them, and out of them. Sometimes they wobble, but they allow God to give them strength. Sometimes they stumble, but they lean on God. Sometimes they fall down, but God helps them get up. They are like heat-seeking missiles: God has shown them the target, and they are locked on to it and cannot take a path that leads away from it.

They are on fire. The flame diminishes from time to time, but it never goes out. They believe first, and then they know, that all things are possible—even the impossible. Crazy faith makes one want to get to the end of the journey to see what God sees and does. It's like water on a newly planted flower that has wilted from the heat.

Crazy faith can infect only those who are open to the Holy Spirit. There has to be an erasure of self, which includes doubt and anxiety, replaced by an openness that allows a person the possibility of receiving a Spirit-transfusion. All of the elements that saturate us because of our being human are replaced by the very Spirit of God, and the person who has been infused by the Spirit is never the same. With crazy faith, God is like a relentless coach, urging us to get up and run on and see what God can do.

It is God's desire for us to live life and live it to the fullest (John 10:10). God doesn't want us to live lives of quiet desperation, especially when we say that we're believers. God wants us to experience that vastness of divine love.

It is a sad reality that too many of us will miss this opportunity to see God at God's best. Because we insist on limiting God and putting God in a box, what we get out of life will be what we put into it. We reap what we sow, and when we act with little divine risk, we realize little divine victory. That is not God's intention. That is not God's will.

God's will is for the world to know how good God is. God put us on the earth not to languish, but rather to thrive. But God did not intend for everyone to thrive in the same way. God wants each of us to thrive in the particular way that God prepared. When we decide to doubt, we miss out. God wants us to believe in the craziest things ever. To help us out, Scripture offers us the testimony of our biblical heroes and "she-roes." Those biblical folks, in those stories on which we were raised, were people who had a vision of how God was in the world. And they took action based on those visions. Their faith carried them, sustained them, and aided them, and it gave us a foundation for our faith. They put their faith into action. Just as God worked for them, God works for us!

Action plus vision equals crazy faith!

chapter 1
why faith?

Without faith, it is impossible to please God,
for whoever would approach him must
believe that he exists and that he
rewards those who seek him.
—Hebrews 11:6, NRSV

I remember stumbling onto that verse. It was as though it had suddenly appeared in the classic chapter on faith. As a child, I had been drilled on the chapter's first verse: "Now faith is the substance of things hoped for, the evidence of things not seen" (Hebrews 11:1, KJV). I never understood it. I just had to memorize it, as we all did. When I got older, I read that verse in the NIV translation: "Now faith is being sure of what we hope for and certain of what we do not see." That made a little more sense, but it still didn't connect with me.

Not until I read Hebrews 11:6, "Without faith it is *impossible* to please God," did the whole idea about faith get my attention.

ⓔ ⓔ ⓔ

Having faith doesn't mean that things are always going to go your way. Having faith, though, means that you have the inner strength and desire to go on, no matter what.

You see what you cannot see. And you see what others cannot see or even perceive.

That "sight" gives an energy that is inexplicable yet powerful. It gives courage that others cannot understand. Sight makes one able to tread water when the life's difficulties seem overwhelming.

That's what the author of Hebrews said: "Now faith is being sure of what we hope for and certain of what we do not see" (Hebrews 11:1). The whole of this chapter makes sense if we understand that one point.

Having faith means that we see with different eyes—not human eyes. Human eyes have finite capacity, but eyes of faith are infinite. Eyes of faith see something bigger than life, against all odds and prevailing opinions.

Recently, there was a woman who was very ill with complications from diabetes. She had been apparently fine one day, and then the next day she fell critically ill to the point of death. She was in a coma, and her vital signs were consistently getting worse. She was put on life support. Some of her children thought that she should be taken off life support and allowed to die peacefully. But one of her children kept saying, "No. She'll be all right. God has told me she'll be all right." Her siblings scoffed and cast her aside as a hopeless, religious romantic, but she held her ground.

Days passed. The woman appeared to be getting worse. Even the doctors were antsy for this case to go one way or the other. But the daughter held fast because she could see what nobody else could.

After three agonizing weeks, something happened. The woman awakened. She was taken off life support and began talking. She had been in the grip of death, and now she was awake, talking, and wanting to eat. Her condition improved daily, and after about ten additional days she was released to go home.

The lone child merely said, "I knew it. I could *see* mom walking around."

Crazy faith.

Faith is not hoping beyond hope. Faith is knowing the One in whom you trust, and moving and acting in a way that says you *know*. There is an assurance that what one knows will come to be. One doesn't know how it will come to be. One just knows that *it will be*. That knowledge also inspires one to work toward what is "seen." Faith is not sitting and waiting. It is moving toward the unseen; it is *working* and planning for what you see and know.

Consider Moses. He could *see* deliverance and the promised land. And although that land wasn't physically in his view as he trudged through the wilderness, he *knew* it existed, because God had told him so. And remember Noah. He could *see* a massive flood. And what about Jesus? He could *see* salvation for God's people. What people saw wasn't there yet, but spiritually it was as good as done. That inner "sight" served as a driver for their actions.

Moses and Noah actually saw what they knew would be. They lived long enough to witness the power of faith-inspired living. Jesus died before he could see what God was going to do and how, which brings us back to Hebrews 11. In Hebrews, the writer carefully lists people who lived by faith, such as Abel, Enoch, Noah, and Abraham, and says, "All these people were still living by faith whey they died. They did not receive the things promised; they only saw them and welcomed them from a distance" (Hebrews 11:13). The writer goes on, mentioning Isaac, Jacob, Joseph, Moses, the crossing of the Red Sea, the destruction of the walls of Jericho, and the work of Rahab (Hebrews 11:17-31).

It's as if the writer of Hebrews has grown excited with his own recollections of what had been accomplished because of great faith: "What more shall I say?" (Hebrews 11:32). There were too many details. Their works were both courageous and incredible, beyond the scope of human understanding and vision. Through faith they conquered kingdoms, administered justice, and obtained promises;

they shut the mouths of lions, quenched the fury of flames, and escaped the edges of the sword (Hebrews 11:33-34). The testimony is impressive. Through faith people became powerful in battle; women received back their dead, raised to life again, while others were tortured, mocked, and flogged (Hebrews 11:35-36). Surely, one would think, all these actions would result in them seeing and tasting the end result, the victory, for which they suffered and believed. But the author says, at the end of the chapter, "These were all commended for their faith, yet none of them received what was promised" (Hebrews 11:39).

Whoa! If that's the case, one might ask, "Do I really *want* to have faith? How could God allow an outcome that doesn't honor our hard work and, frankly, our *faith?*"

That's the crux of the problem. We may not like it, but having faith doesn't mean that things are necessarily going to go our way.

Having faith means that we have the energy to push us forward toward something bigger and better than ourselves. Having faith means that we trust God to be God, whatever that looks like and however it is manifested. Having faith means that we *expect* God to be God, just like we expect an elevator to lift us to the hundredth floor or an airliner to lift us to thirty-three thousand feet. Having faith means we understand that expecting God to be God also means we understand that God's ways are not our ways. We understand that God being God is completely out of our control.

She was a widow and a single mother.

The Bible doesn't say how her husband died, nor does it tell us her name. But she was a woman in trouble, a woman scared and at risk because her dire financial situation was threatening her family.

This single mother was desperate. Creditors would take her sons as slaves to pay debts that she had no money to pay. Then she learned that the prophet Elisha was in town, and she knew that he had been purported to do great things in the name of his God. If ever anyone needed God, she did, and she needed God now.

She was a desperate woman on a desperate mission, and she set out to find Elisha. "Your servant my husband is dead," she cried out from a crowd. "You know that he revered the LORD. But now his creditor is coming to take my two boys as his slaves" (2 Kings 4:1).

Elisha heard her and asked, "How can I help you? Tell me, what do you have in your house?"

"I have nothing there at all," she said, annoyed that this so-called big-time prophet didn't already know that, "except a little oil" (2 Kings 4:2).

A little oil.

You can't do much with "a little oil." If she had oil and flour, she could have made bread and sold it. All she had was a little oil.

Elisha then said an amazing thing, almost as if he hadn't heard her: "Go around and ask all your neighbors for empty jars. Don't ask for just a few. Then go inside and shut the door behind you and your sons. Pour oil into all the jars, and as each is filled, put it to one side" (2 Kings 4:3-4).

For a moment, the woman stood silent and stunned. *Who was this man, and what was wrong with him? Didn't he hear me? Didn't he know what "a little oil" meant?* She got ready to protest, and then words from her husband began to ring in her ear: "There isn't anything God cannot do. God may not do it the way you think it should be done, or when, but God can do all things." Whenever he had said that, she scoffed, but now his words wouldn't leave her. She was at a crossroads. She could doubt that God was God and not even attempt to do what the prophet commanded and so lose her sons to the creditors, or she could trust God and expect God to do the most incredible thing in the most impossible situation.

So she went and did as she was told. She continued to collect the jars because the thought of her sons being taken away and used as slaves hurt her to her heart. "Not on account of my debt will they suffer," she vowed, and so she endured the looks, the stares, and the whispers.

Once inside, the woman and her sons began to fill all the jars with oil. "Where is this oil coming from?" she asked aloud, but she dared not stop. This was clearly a divine moment and something that she would never understand and/or be able to explain. So she continued working, her eyes filling with tears as she realized that there was enough oil to pay her debts and keep her sons from bondage.

This woman had faith. This woman dared to trust God. She *expected* deliverance. She did not stop and waste time by trying to figure out how God would do God's work. She simply believed that God was God and expected God's amazing results. As she worked toward her own deliverance, her belief turned to faith, even though that faith did not include knowing how God works. Her initial faith metamorphosed into crazy faith. The jars were filled and running over, and there was oil left over.

That's called *crazy* faith!

☉ ☉ ☉

We cannot have faith unless we dare to trust God. In order to trust God, we have to rein in our desire to box God in or dissect the divine personality into bite-sized morsels. God is so big. What God does and how God does it are beyond human comprehension.

Trusting God is not risky, because God is a sure thing. Now, God "being a sure thing" doesn't mean that bad things can't happen to us; it simply means that God is always available whenever we call.

Having this kind of faith truly does motivate and give hope. When we identify God as an "always there" God, our attitude about God begins to change. We grow from a childlike faith into a mature faith. Knowing that God is an "always there" God give us a sense of confidence, even in our darkest moments. And that is the relationship we should have with the God who promised "never to leave us" (Deuteronomy 31:6; John 14:18; Hebrews 13:5).

Even worshiping God doesn't mean that there will not be "wilderness moments" or even "wilderness years" when it seems that we cannot find our way. Faith, in those instances, will keep us sane, focused, and comforted in spite of dire circumstances. Scripture says that when we search for God with all our heart and soul, we will find God (Deuteronomy 4:29). And faith means that we understand this and know it to be true.

ⓔ ⓔ ⓔ

Why faith?

Because without faith, it's impossible to please God, and we, because we love God, want to please God.

Having faith gives us the ability to hold on and see what cannot be seen in the most impossible of situations. We can tread water; we can survive and emerge from tough circumstances less bruised than if we enter those circumstances without faith.

Faith acts as a kind of spiritual endorphin, giving energy that is healing and empowering. Faith takes away the fatigue of fighting life's daily battles and gives us strength for the journey.

Faith exists for us, not for God. It's like when my parents used to tell me, "I've already learned that lesson; you have yet to learn it!" We have to choose to trust God, choose to believe in God, and finally, choose to know God. It is in the knowing God that faith is born, and in that birth comes new life for the believer.

And from that faith comes the extraordinary possibility of absolutely crazy faith!

Crazy-Faith Challenge

When in your life did you have a "little oil" moment, and how did you sustain your faith in God? When we have difficulties, sometimes our faith falters, and we get unsteady in our relationship with God. During those times it's hard to believe that nothing is impossible for God. It's hard to have faith in the midst of a storm. Storms do come and uproot our lives, so how do you cope and find strength? People of faith must believe, no matter how crazy and improbable, that their faith will be sustained and rewarded. So when the next crisis hits—and it will—try believing in the impossible, try standing on God's promises and wait to see what God does. Just take a deep breath, and then walk out in crazy faith.

chapter 2
before I be a slave

*I have not the slightest doubt that when that
day comes, truth and justice will prevail.*
—Nelson Mandela

It's one thing to have faith when things are going well; it's quite
another thing to have faith when *nothing* is going well. It really
doesn't matter if one's condition or predicament is of one's own
doing. In that instance, a person can accept responsibility for the
situation and take some of the pressure off God to "fix it." But
when a person is thrown into suffering because of someone else's
actions, and the outcome of those actions is not only unfair but
also painful, it's much harder to have faith, let alone crazy faith,
that things will get better.

Faith cannot be called faith if optimism and hope only exist
when life is humming along just fine, running on all cylinders. But
when we find ourselves in the grip of misery and defeat and yet
still seem to know that the present condition is not the final scene
in the play, that's when we can claim faith—crazy faith. Faith in
general, and crazy faith in particular, allow us to give an affirmative answer to the question "Can anything good come of this?"
As we answer in the affirmative, the senselessness of what we've
just proclaimed escapes us, and we are energized for yet another
day, another try.

The truth of the matter is that we who attend church or profess to be religious are often miffed, even offended and puzzled, when things go not just badly, but very badly. It's hard to hold on and stand firmly in the belief that "God is good all the time" when, even with our faithfulness, God seems to be not so faithful to us.

The problem is that most of us do not practice faith. We hear the stories from the Bible and assume that faith "just comes," when in fact we have to work at beating back our human tendency to give up and at learning how to believe completely in the most abject of times.

The problem comes in how we define God's "faithfulness." Too often, our definition of God being faithful to us means God giving us what we want, with a minimum of angst on our part. We feel that we've already earned brownie points for going to church, singing in the choir, or teaching a Bible study. Then we look around and see non-Christians whose lives are going really well even though, we point out, "they're not doing the right things." It makes us angry, or at least it confuses us. One of the psalms captures the sentiment: "Do not fret because of evil men or be envious of those who do wrong; for like the grass they will soon wither, like green plants they will soon die away" (Psalm 37:1-2).

It seems rather foolhardy to trust in a God who doesn't seem to care about the innocent who lets those who do evil get ahead in life while those who do good suffer. What kind of God is that? It causes us to pause, to gasp for a moment, as we try to make sense out of being religious and holding on. The logical thing to ask, especially if one is suffering, is "For what? Why am I holding on? What's going to change?"

Crazy faith defies logic and rational thought. Some might say that it's downright stupid to keep believing in a God whom one cannot see, especially in light of continuing bad times. We read the Bible and see the word "immediately." Jesus says a prayer or appears in a situation, and "immediately" things change for the better. If that's how Jesus works, why, we wonder, is our deliverance, our answer, our relief taking so long or not coming at all? There seems to be a contradiction between Scripture and reality, and we cannot reconcile what we read and what we experience.

Our confusion moves us farther away from God and even from the desire to practice faith. And most of us are tempted to dismiss the Bible and its stories as myth and poppycock and, like the Israelites, to cling to idols, things we can touch and see, to bring us peace and victory.

Such was not the case, however, with Nelson Mandela.

§ § §

Nelson Mandela was not a religious man. People called him all kinds of things, including a communist, but when asked in 1984 if he was a Christian, Mandela replied, "Very definitely."[1] Biographer Anthony Sampson writes of him, "Mandela was certainly no saint himself, and he would never have a strong religious faith."[2]

Mandela was born in South Africa on July 18, 1918, and was named "Rolihlahla"—the son of Hendry and Nosekeni Mandela. Although his father never became a Christian, his mother did, and she had her son baptized as a Methodist at the age of seven. That was when he was given the name "Nelson."[3] He went to school and studied to become a lawyer. In 1952 he and his friend Oliver Tambo established the first African law firm in the country in Johannesburg. Their office was located in an area of the city that was for whites only, but they stayed there illegally until 1961.[4]

For reasons that are painfully obvious, Mandela hated apartheid. His father had been a chief, for the legacy of his family was one of royalty. Mandela was a proud man and could never accept the indignity of South Africa's racist laws. His work as an attorney was spent advocating on behalf of black Africans, as well as colored and Indians, who were being treated unjustly by the apartheid government. Although the government set up road-blocks to keep them "under control" and limit the numbers of victories that they could secure for clients, Mandela and Tambo never strayed from their calling.

Mandela was a young man in the 1950s when something happened that began to change his life's course. The South African government passed the "Suppression of Communism Act." At the heart of the government's action was its distaste of communist principles, which advocated equality between the races. The Suppression of Communism Act effectively shut down the ability of races to interrelate, amounting to a ban on free speech. Blacks, coloreds, Indians, and, of course, communists were outraged and began to organize to protest the passing of the bill.[5]

The cooperating groups created the "Defend Free Speech Convention" and planned a one-day strike on May Day. Young people, including Mandela, were energized and worked to make the event successful. A huge crowd, reportedly ten thousand people, jammed Market Square for the event.[6]

That May Day strike changed Mandela's life forever. As he was walking home in the black township of Orlando with his friend Walter Sisulu, watching a group of peaceful protestors, mounted police charged into the crowd and opened fire. Mandela and Sisulu hid in a dormitory, and by the end of the evening, eighteen black people had been killed.[7]

That experience stirred up Mandela's sense of responsibility to all African people. When the African National Congress (ANC) met in December 1951, and committed to fight "six unjust laws," Mandela was on board.[8] He listened as the leaders of the ANC outlined the campaign. If the government refused to get rid of the six unjust laws, the ANC would lead the people in a "Defiance Campaign," an activity in which people would practice civil disobedience, similar to the strategy led by Ghandi in India.

And then Mandela's life took a turn from which he would never backtrack. From the outset, his commitment to the ANC and its cause was firm. His faith that their actions could make a difference never wavered. As the Defiance Campaign got underway, Mandela found himself supported by masses of black people who were being treated unfairly. Despite all the setbacks that Mandela experienced, he recognized that "oppressed people and the oppressors are at loggerheads."[9] But he was steadfast in believing that things would change for the better. He said, "I have not the slightest doubt that when that day comes truth and justice will prevail."[10] "The feelings of the oppressed people have never been more bitter....To overthrow oppression has been sanctioned by humanity and is the highest aspiration of every free man."[11]

Surely, his faith statements were muted by the realities around him. The more the ANC fought against oppression, the more the government increased its attack on the move for freedom. The ANC drew up a "Freedom Charter," which gave their movement direction and strengthened their sense of purpose. The charter stated that South African people were on a quest to make a "democratic, nonracial South Africa."[12] The preamble to the document said that the black people of South Africa had goals and that the people should and would govern, all national groups would have equal rights and would share in the country's wealth, and the land would be shared among those who worked it.[13]

In response, the government made the work of Mandela and the ANC more difficult. Despite feelings of hopelessness, Mandela fought on. And he became a leader in the movement because his commitment to fight oppression was so complete and so resolute.

The government eventually charged Mandela with high treason and with conspiracy to overthrow the state.[14] In December of 1956 he was arrested along with 155 other people who had been working tirelessly in the movement. The process of dealing with these changes began in 1956 and did not end until 1961. The actual trial began on August 3, 1959. Even as the trial commenced, the work of the ANC did not stop. Mandela and the others were out of jail and could now participate in all of the demonstrations.

The attention given to the ANC might have been part of the reason behind the birth of yet another political organization, the Pan Africanist Congress (PAC), which competed with the ANC and opposed the ANC's position or belief in multiracialism. The PAC did not think that the ANC was militant enough. Emergence of the PAC seriously compromised the work of the ANC. Even with the treason trial hanging overhead, the PAC sought to be a voice, and in 1960 it called for a campaign to protest the law requiring nonwhites over the age of sixteen to carry passes. It was in direct competition with an antipass campaign already established by the ANC. Mandela was not happy. "They knew of the ANC's antipass campaign and had been invited to join, but instead of linking arms with the Congress movement, they sought to sabotage us."[15] The PAC slated its campaign to begin ten days before the ANC's campaign. For the most part, the response to the PAC was minimal, but things were very different in Sharpeville.

PAC workers had organized the people, and by early afternoon "several thousand surrounded the police station," Mandela wrote.[16] He continued: "The demonstrators were controlled and unarmed. A police force of seventy-five was greatly outnumbered and panicky. No one heard warning shots or an order to shoot, but suddenly, the police opened fired on the crowd and continued to shoot, as the demonstrators turned and ran in fear....It was a massacre, and the next day press photos displayed the savagery on the front pages around the world."[17]

It was a dark time. Optimism for justice was not high.

Finally, it was time for the verdict. The court ruled that it was "impossible...to come to the conclusion that the ANC had acquired or adopted a policy to overthrow the state by violence."[18] The ruling also said that the prosecution had "failed to prove that the ANC was a Communist organization or that the Freedom Charter envisioned a Communist state."[19]

Mandela was elated but not fooled. His political philosophy began to shift from being nonviolent to violent. The massacre at Sharpeville had daunted his belief that nonviolence would work in South Africa. The stance called for him to go underground for his own safety. The South African government, embarrassed by the verdict in the treason trial, was out to get him and others whom they felt were threatening the status quo of the apartheid regime. Mandela was dubbed the "Black Pimpernel," akin to the fictional "Scarlet Pimpernel," who had been able to evade capture during the French Revolution.[20] After being underground for more than a year, he was arrested and again put on trial, this time charged with inciting African workers to strike and with leaving the country without valid travel documents.[21] He was convicted and sentenced to five years in prison with no parole.

While he was in prison, the police raided a farm where ANC members were known to meet and strategize. Although no weapons were found, police discovered a document entitled "Operation Mayibuye," a plan for guerilla warfare in South Africa.[22] Mandela was thought to be behind it, and he and others received additional, more serious charges of sabotage and conspiracy that were punishable by death. They were essentially charged with trying to overthrow the government.

At the trial, the judge was irritated with the prosecution's fumbling of the case. The closed session essentially cleared Mandela and the others on the charges, but before they could leave the courtroom, they were rearrested for sabotage and returned to jail. They pleaded not guilty as their new trial resumed, but knew that the odds were against an acquittal.

On Friday, June 12, 1964, they appeared before the judge as the sentence was read. Judge Quartus de Wet read the findings of the court: "The function of this court…is to enforce the laws of the state within which it functions. The crime of which the accused have been convicted, that is the main crime, the crime of conspiracy, is in essence one of high treason. The state has decided not to charge the crime in this form. Bearing this in mind, and giving the matter very serious consideration, I have decided not to impose the supreme penalty…but consistent with my duty that is the only leniency I can show. The sentence in the case of all the accused will be one of life imprisonment."[23]

Thus began Mandela's sojourn on Robben Island.

To one not gifted with faith, prison seems to be the end of life. Mandela, by his own admission, was not "religious." In fact, he saw a distinct separation between being religious and being political. The difference for him was stark. Mandela's faith, says Anthony Sampson, was a matter of speculation. He believed in religious, Christian principles, chief among them being forgiveness and human dignity. "But he was not a formal believer like Oliver Tambo; he did not quote the Bible or discuss theology."[24]

And yet, Mandela did have faith. After his conviction and life sentence in prison, he and the others were taken back to Robben Island. He was thrown into a cell in Section B of the prison, the isolation section, which was eight feet by seven feet. It had a small, barred window, and he was given a flimsy mat that he would place on the often-damp floor on which to sleep, along with three thin blankets. It was where he lived for the next eighteen years.[25]

But he never lost faith. Walter Sisulu, who was imprisoned at Robben Island along with Mandela, said, "We never lost confidence.…We had confidence in ideas."[26] Mandela himself wrote in 1975, "In my lifetime I shall step out into the sunshine, walk with firm feet."[27]

How he could say that, with such certainty, given the conditions under which he and the others lived, is beyond reason. It was simply crazy for him to believe that he would get out of prison, given the sentence, the gravity of the accusations, the power of the government and its animosity toward his cause, and the wretched conditions in which he was forced to live.

The living conditions on Robben Island were oppressive, designed to burden the soul and sap resolve. One prisoner, Eddie Daniels, who was "a light skinned colored liberal," found the conditions almost too much to bear, but he said that whenever he felt demoralized, he hugged Mandela and Sisulu, and "their strength would flow into me. We couldn't see a future—it was blank. But Mandela always could."[28]

Mandela's faith seemed to be fueled by a poem that he frequently quoted and taught to others. "Invictus," by W. E. Henley, reads: "It matters not how strait the gate, / How charged with punishments the scroll, / I am the master of my fate; / I am the captain of my soul."[29]

Mandela's capacity for faith, the energy and drive that he was able to pull from his faith, allowed him to be a leader even while in prison. He did not languish in prison, but he did miss many milestones. He was in prison when his mother died, and when his firstborn son was killed in a motorcycle accident, and in both cases he was denied the privilege of attending their funerals. He mourned that his children had grown up not knowing him. When he saw them again, they were grown with children of their own. He suffered, but he held fast.

When finally there was a stirring, when the winds of freedom began to move in Mandela's direction, he was emotionally and spiritually able to feel the change. The world was not pleased with South Africa. Apartheid had become unpopular, and the world was reacting in the best and most effective way it could: economic sanctions. Most world leaders were in support of Mandela. His faith drove him—faith that his cause was right, faith that he would be released from prison along with all his friends and co-workers, faith that apartheid in South Africa would end. *He always had faith.*

As the pressure of the world community began to impact South Africa, Mandela found himself talking about release from prison. Miracles began to happen. President Frederik Willem de Klerk called for reconciliation between the ANC and the South African government. Bans were lifted, and troops left the townships. De Klerk, who was a religious man, told his brother, who was a supporter of ending apartheid, "It was as if God had taken a hand—a new turn in world history."[30]

Finally on February 2, 1990, de Klerk delivered the speech that affirmed Mandela's faith. "In a few minutes, de Klerk reversed nearly all of his predecessors' policies over the past three decades. All political organizations, including the ANC and the South African Communist Party, would be legalized. All political prisoners not guilty of violent crimes would be released. All executions would be suspended." And the government had taken "a firm decision to release Mandela unconditionally."[31]

The war was not yet over, but a decisive battle had definitely been won. Mandela, who always believed that he would walk out of prison "on firm feet," did so.

It took twenty-seven years—some ten thousand days in jail.

Crazy-Faith Challenge

When I visited Robben Island and saw the tiny cell in which Nelson Mandela lived for eighteen years, I shuddered. Would I have held on? Would you? Would my faith have been strong enough to stubbornly cling to a belief that God is good all the time?

How would you have survived? Mandela's faith is an extreme, positive example of what belief in God and crazy faith can do. It really did take an unbelievable act to believe that faith could trump racial hatred. It was crazy to believe that the whole world would latch onto the antiapartheid movement. It was crazy for Mandela to believe that he could initiate the spark of democracy. And it was seriously crazy for Mandela even to imagine becoming the nation's first black president. But he did. Crazy.

In the midst of a situation like Mandela's, when all seems lost, do you think that your faith would triumph over your fears and doubts? So try being crazy for a moment, and imagine having just a portion, an ounce, of the faith that Mandela had, and then step out of the way and let God be God.

chapter 3
God's ridiculous expectations

Then Moses stretched out his hand over the sea.
The LORD drove the seas back by a strong east
wind all night, and turned the sea to dry land;
and the waters were divided.
—Exodus 14:21, NRSV

God expected ridiculous things out of Moses.

Moses led a privileged life as the adopted grandson of the very same Pharaoh who wanted to kill him and other Israelite boys. But God also allowed Moses' own biological mother to nurse him, and undoubtedly it was she who instilled in him a sense of his identity as a Hebrew—one of God's people. Moses' first attempts to "save" the people of his birth resulted in the death of an Egyptian. Moses had a sense of his future, and he came to understand the ridiculous things that God would require. God made it clear, speaking from a burning bush, that Moses was being called to deliver the people of Israel out of slavery, through the wilderness and into the freedom of the land promised generations before to Abraham.

◉ ◉ ◉

God's expectations of Moses were indeed ridiculous. So Moses believed that the ridiculous was possible. Many of Moses' obstacles were limitations that he perceived in himself. He didn't know God all that well, and he certainly didn't have much knowledge of the Hebrew patriarchs and God's acts in their lives. Moses had been raised as an Egyptian, not as a leader among the Hebrews. And he couldn't speak very well.

God addressed all of Moses' concerns, so Moses went to see the Pharaoh armed only with a staff in his hand and God's words in his mouth. As ill-equipped as Moses was, God expected him to demand the release of thousands of Hebrew slaves. Talk about seriously crazy faith!

By the time Moses and the Israelites journeyed into the wilderness, fleeing from the Pharaoh, they had had plenty of opportunities to see how God worked. But now came a moment when Moses' crazy faith would be tested. He had seen God do the impossible, but still he was bound by limited human vision. Although God pushed Moses to believe more in what he could not see or imagine, and Moses had come a long way in the struggle to accept God's power, what he was about to witness would jostle even his faith.

Moses and the Israelites were running through a brutal wilderness and away from people who wanted to capture or kill them. They were tired, scared, and hungry, and there was nowhere to go. And Pharaoh's army was still coming. Wearily, Moses and the Israelites trudged on their way, and God was with them. By day, the LORD "went ahead of them in a pillar of cloud to guide them on their way and by night in a pillar of fire to give them light" (Exodus 13:21). Never did the pillar of cloud or fire leave them. There was still the Red Sea in front of them. Though Moses dared not ask God how this journey would end for the Israelites, he was truly worried.

When God speaks, it is not what Moses expected: "Tell the Israelites to turn back and encamp near Pi Hahiroth, between Migdol and the sea. They are to encamp by the sea, directly opposite Baal Zephon" (Exodus 14:2). Moses groaned. The people had already given him a hard time because God was leading them on a longer route, along the desert.

But God had a reason. God told Moses that if they followed this plan, Pharaoh would think that they were confused and had lost their way, and that they were ripe for capture because they were hemmed in by the desert on one side and by the sea on the other side. God would harden the heart of Pharaoh, who in turn would savagely pursue the Israelites. God paused long enough to give Moses time to take in what was being said: "I will harden Pharaoh's heart and he will pursue....But I will gain glory for myself through Pharaoh and all his army, and the Egyptians will know that I am the LORD" (Exodus 14:4).

It was ridiculous for God to expect the Israelites to believe in this tactic. It was ridiculous for God to expect Moses to deliver this message to the people with conviction. Moses knew exactly what would happen. Pharaoh would muster his finest soldiers and military equipment. He took six hundred of his best chariots and all the other Egyptian chariots as well. He pursued the Israelites with a joyful vengeance. Finally, he thought, this game will be over. There will be nowhere for the Israelites to go.

The Israelites realized the gravity of the situation, and they began to complain. In terror, they asked Moses, "Was it because there were no graves in Egypt that you brought us to the desert to die? What have you done to us by bringing us out of Egypt? Didn't we say to you in Egypt, 'Leave us alone; let us serve the Egyptians'? It would have been better for us to serve the Egyptians than to die in the desert!" (Exodus 14:11-12).

Moses knew that he had to reassure the people that God was still with them. Moses had to remind the people that God loved them and wanted them free. "Do not be afraid," he said. "Stand firm and you will see the deliverance the LORD will bring you this day. The Egyptians you see today you will never see again. The LORD will fight for you; you need only to be still" (Exodus 14:13-14).

He said it, but he didn't know how it would ever come to be.

In desperation, Moses cried out to God. By this time, they had reached the Red Sea. They could hear the hooves of the horses of Pharaoh's approaching army. Behind were soldiers ready to slaughter them, and ahead was water ready to drown them. And over them was God.

"Raise your staff and stretch your hand over the sea," God commanded Moses (Exodus 14:16).

Oh, that's going to do a lot of good, Moses must have thought. God's expectation that the staff would make it possible for the Israelites to cross the sea seemed ridiculous. Moses had good reason to think that way. Although there is debate on whether this body of water was the modern-day Red Sea or lake called the "Sea of Reeds," crossing any body of water to elude capture would have been daunting. In either case, this body of water was huge, but the intent was to show that God was bigger than the Israelites' biggest obstacle.

"Raise your staff and stretch your hand over the sea to divide the water so that the Israelites can go through the sea on dry ground" (Exodus 14:16).

It was a critical moment for Moses. On the one hand, he faced the vast body of water with only a nondescript staff in his hand. It was crazy to expect that raising it toward the sea would make an ounce of difference. And how would God make the ground beneath the sea dry? Was God testing him?

On the other hand, disobeying God would send the wrong message to the One who had led the Israelites through all kinds of danger. Whom did Moses trust more? Himself or his God? God had given assurances that Pharaoh would not be a problem and that the Egyptians would know that Moses' God was the Lord (Exodus 14:18). But were God's assurances enough to trump Moses' human inclination to doubt?

It was a crazy-faith moment. Moses had little time to vacillate. He either believed or he didn't. He would show God either that he trusted God fully or that his was a faith with stipulations. The Israelites were whining and scared. The desert sun was hot, and his group's supplies were running low. What would Moses do?

As he stood there, the "angel of God, who had been traveling in front of Israel's army, withdrew and went behind them" (Exodus 14:19). The pillar of cloud also moved behind them. Moses watched, interested. What was God doing? Now, in front of them was the obstacle, and behind them was God, giving light and protection. Throughout the night, the story goes, "The Cloud was now between the camp of Egypt and the camp of Israel. The Cloud enshrouded one camp in darkness and flooded the other with light. The two camps didn't come near each other all night." (Exodus 14:20, THE MESSAGE). Moses had to feel God's presence. He had to feel God trying to gently remind him that no matter how ridiculous, "God was in it."

So, Moses stretched out his hand over the sea. As he stood there holding the staff, he could feel the wind. That was not unusual. In the desert, there were often windy nights and serious winds that caused huge dust storms. So as the wind increased, Moses thought nothing of it. After a long while, Moses dropped his arm and moved toward the camp. He found a spot of grass, wrapped himself in a blanket, and went to sleep.

He awoke to shouts coming from the camp. What was it? Were the Egyptians here? Had they already taken people captive? What was he going to say? How was he going to explain this to this restless, restive people? But as he moved toward their shouts, he realized that they were not shouting in agony or anger—they sounded surprised. Moses did not understand what had happened until he got to the sea.

Those winds, the very ones that Moses dismissed as routine, had been the hand of God. A strong east wind had driven the sea back. "The waters were divided" (Exodus 14:21).

In front of Moses were two huge walls of water, one on the right, one on the left. And the pathway between them was dry. The ground was *dry*. It was a miracle, but Moses halted. This was a wonderful sight, but it was scary. What if those walls of water gave out as the Israelites made their way through to the other side? Moses looked at the water; it was *so* high. But God had promised to make a way. And God's word turned out to be true.

But did God really expect them to trust enough to walk this path with all that water on both sides?

Moses' trepidation was echoed by the Israelites. "I hope that Moses isn't thinking that we're going in there," he heard. "I'm not going to drown. I'll go back to Egypt. In fact, I'll just let them capture me. I'm not going to die out here." Some even backed away from the shore.

Moses could understand, but God had kept the promise. Some crazy faith!

"Do it," Moses told himself. "Just start walking." As Moses walked, the sound of the water frightened him. The dry ground amazed him, but he couldn't really appreciate all that he saw. It was as if there were two giant hands coaxing the water to stay in place. "God is in it," his spirit whispered to him, and so Moses began to walk, slowly, deliberately, and the people began to follow.

Tears were running down Moses' face, because he was amazed at God's power and because he was terrified. He could still hear the Egyptians. They were following the Israelites. Would they all die as the waters grew tired and came rushing down, killing them all instantly?

They continued to walk. The pillars of cloud and of fire were still behind the Israelites. When they finally reached the other side, some sobbed, and others stood on the bank and looked back at walls of water. Moses kept his face upward, so only God could see his tears. The Egyptians were still coming.

But "during the last watch of the night the LORD looked down from the pillar of cloud and fire at the Egyptian army and threw it into confusion. He made the wheels of their chariots come off so that they had difficulty driving. And the Egyptians said, 'Let's get away from the Israelites! The LORD is fighting for them against Egypt!'" (Exodus 14:25).

All the noise jarred Moses from his mood, and he looked back toward the sea and could see only scurrying men and animals. He was puzzled. He hadn't seen what God had done.

But God spoke to him, "Stretch out your hand over the sea so that the waters may flow back over the Egyptians and their chariots and horsemen" (Exodus 14:26). *Stretch out your hand.* This time, Moses didn't doubt. He had heard that command before, but this time was different. His eyes had seen what God could do. It had been a crazy command. Connected with the command had been God's expectation that Moses would obey and believe. Even now, Moses did not understand how the sea had parted. He did not understand how his hand and a staff carried out God's purposes. He knew only that they had been on the brink of capture and now they were free.

He stretched out his hand.

The Egyptians died, the great walls of water folding over them, and in seconds their terrified shrieks could no longer be heard. It was over. The waters were calm, as if nothing had happened.

God had expected Moses to believe in the ridiculous. And Moses had been able to see the ridiculous and the impossible carried out.

Crazy-Faith Challenge

When I was first divorced, I had to have faith that I could make it with two young children on a pastor's small salary. There was daycare to pay for, credit-card bills, food, diapers, and at the time, two mortgages. I was at the shore of my Red Sea. I cried and worried, and then God told me to have faith. It was so hard to believe. But God was God, and I could not preach what I did not practice. Eventually, my Red Sea parted. And the bills were paid.

All of us have had those Red Sea experiences. The question is: When your Red Sea experience comes, how will you handle it? Will you look at the walls of water on the pathway that God provides and have the faith to walk through, or will you give in to doubt and be trampled by the enemies of joy and peace?

The problem for us comes when we limit God to what *we* see, think, or imagine. A person operating strictly from the intellect will not receive this Red Sea story. He or she will find all the reasons that the events could not have happened. But crazy faith demands that we believe in God's ridiculous expectations.

"Stretch out your hand."

chapter 4
roses and a key

If I wanted something, whatever it was, I could.
—Chris Gardner

I read a story about a beloved pastor who was known for preaching great sermons about faith. His congregants were taken with his insight, and his words inspired many. Then it happened that his only daughter, a young woman who had been the joy of his life, was killed in a car accident. She had recently graduated from college and was engaged to be married. Her sudden loss was devastating for all who loved her. But for the father, her death was catastrophic.

This same man who eloquently taught on faith now was distraught to the point of severe depression. He could not function. He could not eat or engage in his normal daily activities, nor could he preach or teach. He eventually resigned from the ministry.

Later, he admitted that he had never experienced huge pain or loss in his life. He had understood intellectually what faith was, and he understood it in terms of asking God for something and believing that God would respond. But when it came to his personal grief, he was so angry with God that he got lost in the pain. A part of him believed that God was good and would get him through this storm. But a greater part of him couldn't even find God. He never returned to the ministry.

This man came to understand that faith is a gift. The apostle Paul identifies that kind of faith in 1 Corinthians 12:7-11, where he talks about the gifts of the Spirit. If Paul is to be believed, not everyone has the same capacity to believe, because we all have different gifts. From a Christian perspective, acquiring the gift of faith comes from keeping one's eyes on God. When Peter walked on the water, he was doing well until he began to focus on the power of the wind (Matthew 14:30). It was then that he became afraid and began to sink.

Fear and faith can cancel each other out.

So if crazy faith is what you seek, you cannot be afraid. You have to work to find ways to keep your eyes and thoughts on Jesus and not on the logical reasons why it would make better sense not to believe. When you move from fear to faith, the troubles that beat against the spirit lose power.

Having that gift involves being "anchored in the Lord." Periodically, one of our church soloists brings the congregation to tears singing "My Soul Has Been Anchored in the Lord." As soon as Deacon Chuck Jordan begins, handkerchiefs come out and tears flow.

The song is a declaration of faith, a faith that keeps us anchored and sane while we are facing our Red Sea crossings. When we talk about having crazy faith during a Red Sea moment, that's the kind of faith that most of us do not have.

Not unless we are someone like Chris Gardner.

◎ ◎ ◎

The movie *The Pursuit of Happyness* is the story of entrepreneur Chris Gardner, his struggles with homelessness and as a committed father. The story of Gardner (played brilliantly by Will Smith in the movie) had me wondering if I would have been able to stand in his situation.

But when I read the book *The Pursuit of Happyness*, there was no doubt in my mind that I don't have that kind of faith. Just think of it: a single, homeless, jobless man, who for a whole year bundled his son up and carted him around in a stroller, with some plastic from the dry cleaners to shield him against the rain. If ever a person had crossed the Red Sea, Chris Gardner had.

By his own admission, Gardner had been on the banks of a Red Sea his whole life. Gardner had "lived in a series of houses, walk-ups, and flats, punctuated by intermittent separations and stays with a series of relatives, all within a four-block area."[1] He survived the trials of his childhood, but not without some life-changing words from his mother. One day he was watching basketball on television and said out loud that those basketball players would one day make a million dollars. His mother heard him and said, "Son, if you want to, one day *you* could make a million dollars."[2] Her words represented a turning point in Gardner's life, reminding him, "If I wanted something, whatever it was, I could."[3]

He continued to believe her words, especially "in those moments pushing up the hills in the downpour with my son looking up at me from his stroller through rain-splattered dry-cleaning plastic, and in the desolate hours when the only place of refuge was in a BART station bathroom."[4]

Gardner's "year from hell" began suddenly. He had been working as a research assistant for a prominent San Francisco doctor. When Gardner graduated from high school, he enlisted in the Navy and became a competent medic. His skills did not go unnoticed by doctors with whom he worked, and he was hired to set up a lab and became a research assistant. Gardner was so talented that doctors at the University of San Francisco's medical school had him train medical students and interns in specific procedures, and he co-authored papers with Dr. Bob Ellis that appeared in prominent medical journals.[5]

Gardner was happy for a while. He had gotten married. But he also found that his interest in medical school—something on which his wife had planned—was waning. He was sensing the world and its possibilities, and he regretted having gotten married too soon. Then, he began a relationship with the woman who became the mother of his son, Christopher, and later his daughter, Jacintha.

One day, he saw a man driving a red Ferrari 308, and he was struck by the car's beauty. Gardner decided that he would own one. Gardner asked the car's owner what he did for a living. He was a stockbroker who made $80,000 a month. Curious, Gardner asked the man about his profession. The job description struck a chord with Gardner, and the thought of being a stockbroker hounded him. Gardner quit his current job just as he landed one at E. F. Hutton. But when he arrived for the new job that following Monday, the person who hired him had quit, so Gardner no longer had a job.

From there, things went from bad to worse. He found odd jobs, but he didn't make nearly enough to support his family. He was separated from his wife and was living with his lover. The new baby put a strain on his lover—her ambitions and finances were stretched. She wanted him to get a "real job." And she had no faith that he could make it as a stockbroker. Stockbrokers had bachelor's degrees and MBAs. Gardner had neither. She and Gardner fought, and she called the police to the house and was ready to press charges against him, but she never got the chance. When Gardner went looking for stockbroker jobs, he piled up parking tickets. When the police ran his plates, they discovered that he owed $1,200 in parking fines.

Gardner was arrested, but he didn't have the money to pay the tickets, so he was sentenced to ten days in jail. But even in the midst of legal problems, Gardner hadn't forgotten to try to get another interview, this one at Dean Witter. A friend at the firm arranged the meeting for the morning after he was to be released. He managed to get the interview rescheduled for the next day. Once out of jail, though, Gardner realized that his lover had taken their baby son and left. The house was empty, and there was no money to pay the rent. Gardner was homeless.

All he had was what he'd worn to jail. But he still had to show up for the interview. When he arrived, the interviewer thought that he was a delivery boy. Gardner told the interviewer the truth, and to his surprise, his future boss, Mr. Albanese, commiserated with him. At the end of their time together, Albanese told Gardner to be at the firm Monday morning. Gardner was now an intern, training to be a stockbroker. He was on his way.

There was only one thing wrong. He didn't have his son. Little Chris was with his mother, and Gardner didn't know where. He no longer had a place to live, though that didn't bother him. But it hurt not to know where his son was. He bunked at the home of friends, and sometimes, because often he was the last one to leave the office, under his desk. He decided to make the best of a bad situation, and though he worried about not having his son, he kept up with his class work at Dean Witter.

With his work complete, he passed the test that qualified him as a neophyte stockbroker. It had been four long months, with no son, no money, and no place to live. Then the mother of his son appeared. She realized that being a single mom was too much, so she left little Chris with his dad. Gardner was elated, but he was also struck now with the realization that he really was homeless. The rooming houses where he stayed did not take children, and he didn't feel comfortable imposing on friends with a little boy who was not yet toilet trained.

Like Moses, Gardner was facing his Red Sea. And like the widow whom Elisha helped, he had no jars and no oil with which to prepare food for survival. And yet, he was driven by his faith, which said that he *would* make it and make it big, if he kept going.

He found a room at The Palms, a hotel populated by prostitutes. Although it was far from ideal for the father and his young son, it was a roof over their heads. As summer turned into fall and fall into winter, he made adjustments: "I cut back on everything, making sure I carried all our stuff with me every day, juggling the duffel bag, the briefcase, my hanging bag, the Pampers box, and an umbrella as I moved downstream from The Palms where a room and a color television cost $25 a night to a trucker motel that got us a room and black-and-white TV for $10 a day."[6]

One night, they slept outside at Golden Gate Park because he had spent the motel money on food and drink for little Chris. Other times, they slept in the men's bathroom at the BART station. He became familiar with San Francisco in ways most of us could never imagine. He knew the cracks in the roads and the worst hills, those with the steepest grades, and he avoided them because they were too difficult to navigate with the stroller. Clearly, he had every reason to give up.

But he also had crazy faith, and so he didn't give up. Chris just kept going, believing that there was a way out and that he was headed toward it. Then he heard about a hotel for the homeless, operated by Glide Memorial Church. He had attended services at Glide, and the pastor, Rev. Cecil Williams, had noticed him. When Williams heard about Gardner's situation, he told him about the hotel. Chris was more than glad. It was a sign that things were getting better. Sometimes he didn't make it back in time to get a room, and no one ever got the same room, but at least it was clean and made it possible for him to save the money that he'd been spending on cheap hotels and motels.

His faith fed him. "Every Sunday in church, as I prayed to find my way out of the problems of this period, I just knew that if I could hold on, everything would be so fine I'd never have a care in the world after that."[7] He looked for light in the darkness, and often he found it. Staying at the hotel for the homeless allowed him to save money to put his son in daycare. Every morning he gathered up his son and all their belongings and headed toward the daycare because he still had to be at work on time. Taking the bus wasn't an option. So they walked, his son in the stroller, with Pampers, a duffel bag, and a briefcase—all their possessions. "As long as I could stay in the light, figuratively speaking, by keeping my focus on what I could control, worry and fear were kept at bay," he said.[8]

Staying "in the light" is a requirement for keeping the faith. There are many deterrents and many justifiable reasons to give up. Impatience and weariness can set in, and time goes slowly. Gardner says that while he was homeless, shuffling back and forth over the streets and sidewalks of San Francisco, he could hear the taunting voice of his stepfather asking him who the hell he thought he was. *Maybe my stepfather was right*, Gardner thought during this time. *Maybe he had been right all along.*

But then there were angels that he didn't expect—for example, hookers who would slip little Chris $5 from time to time. Gardner noticed that they loved his son and were more than willing to help, so he'd take the money, which allowed them to eat. Then there was Williams, who showed Gardner that there were honest clergy in the world who cared. It was something he needed to see.

Then one day Gardner was walking with his son when he passed by a house that had a rose bush on the front lawn. The sight startled him. Who had roses in the ghetto? Had they been there all along, and he just missed them? As he marveled at the roses, he also noticed that the house looked empty. There was an old man sweeping the sidewalk, and Gardner asked if the house was for rent. The old man said, "It could be."[9] The man showed Gardner the inside. He was elated as he walked through, seeing a living room, dining room, and a room that could be a bedroom for little Chris. He began to fantasize about getting away from the hotel and having a permanent place for his son.

The Red Sea was parting.

The old man agreed to let Gardner rent the house. Homelessness was behind him and was going to be swallowed up by this intervention. Gardner got this break "not long before Easter, a celebration of rebirth and resurrection, a time of new beginnings, new roads."[10] He had been on the streets for a year. It had been hard, discouraging, depressing, and disorganized. It had been a time when Gardner, in order to keep going, had to draw on inner resources that he didn't even know he possessed. It had been a time when sometimes he withdrew to let the tears roll down his cheeks, so that little Chris wouldn't see. It had been a time he never thought he'd have to go through. And at times, he thought it would never end.

But then, one day, he saw a rose bush in the ghetto. The Red Sea opened, and Gardner and little Chris walked on dry land.

◉ ◉ ◉

One of the things that made the most impact on Gardner after he got his house was the fact that he had a key. For a year, he'd had no key, no space to call his own. Now, he had a key. And he said that the key was the physical evidence of movement out of suffering toward success. "The key was like the key to the kingdom, a symbol of having made it this far, all the way from where I had been, at the absolute bottom of the hole, to where I was now—an incredible transition."[11]

Crazy-Faith Challenge

Gardner went on to become a wealthy man, succeeding in the investment industry and eventually starting his own firm. But his experience being homeless and having to struggle to hold on to his faith changed his perspective and definition of wealth.

Gardner's wealth lies in the fact that he raised two healthy children as a single parent and was there for them even in the rough times. His wealth can be measured by the fact that he didn't abandon his dreams even when life's storms raged. Instead, he counted his blessings and maintained what he says was an "attitude of gratitude with which we remind ourselves every day to count our blessings."[12] How many of us can say that we have that kind of faith? How many of us would keep going when life's hits just keep coming?

Chris Gardner was one man who had crazy, crazy faith! Caught in a Red Sea experience, he waded through with faith as his anchor.

chapter 5
you're not the boss of me!

David said to Saul, "Let no one lose heart
on account of this Philistine;
your servant will go and fight him."
—1 Samuel 17:32, NRSV

When my children were little, I would hear them arguing.
Caroline would tell Charlie, her little brother, to do or not do
something. And Charlie would protest loudly, saying, "You're not
the boss of me!"

Charlie would proceed to do whatever he wanted. His sense of
independence was growing, and Caroline, who often had been
trying to spare Charlie from something catastrophic, would resign
herself to the reality that her brother was going to get in trouble.
But Charlie would stand firm and proclaim again, "You're not the
boss of me!"

It was amusing to watch and to hear. Actually, I loved it. The
childlike faith that Charlie demonstrated is what God asks of us
and what is required in order to claim crazy faith. A child doesn't
know that something is impossible. Children believe in the impossible. If you tell a child that there was a major flood and a five-
hundred-year-old man built an ark for two of every kind of ani-
mal species, that child simply believes. Adults would interrupt and
bombard the storyteller with a series of questions, searching for a

logical and rational answer. Adults allow their questions and doubts to become their "boss."

Not so with children. They are sponges, soaking in the most delightful of life's possibilities. Nothing is impossible to them. Jesus referred to it in the book of Matthew, when the disciples asked him, "Who is the greatest in the kingdom of heaven?" Calling a child to him, Jesus answered, "I tell you the truth, unless you change and become like little children, you will never enter the kingdom of heaven. Therefore, whoever humbles himself like this child is the greatest in the kingdom of heaven" (Matthew 18:1-4). In the Gospel of Mark, Jesus' appreciation for the faith of children is found yet again: "People were bringing little children to Jesus to have him touch them, but the disciples rebuked them. When Jesus saw this, he was indignant. He said to them, 'Let the little children come to me, and do not hinder them, for the kingdom of God belongs to such as these'" (Mark 10:13-14).

Adults, for all their wisdom, are not really bright when it comes to things of the spirit. They rely too much on what they can see and understand. But little children are different. Their eyes fill with the wonderment of a new day's discovery. They simply believe and imagine the possibilities. That's the essence of having faith: believing in something so strongly even when others doubt.

But it's the child's imagination that leads to faith, and it's a child's faith that feeds the imagination. A child searches for God and believes in good. As a toddler, Charlie was always looking for God. We had told him that God is everywhere, but the concept puzzled him. Nevertheless, he believed and continued to search.

And Charlie was successful, at least in his mind. There were two occasions when Charlie declared that he had seen God. I was holding him in my arms one day, standing on the front porch at bedtime waiting to say goodnight to his dad. As we talked to his father, Charlie's head kept turning toward someone. A drunken man was staggering down the street, mumbling and singing. I had just told Charlie that God was everywhere. As the man got closer and became more visible, Charlie pointed his finger toward the man and said, "There he is! There's God!" Startled, the man turned and went back the way he'd come.

The next time Charlie saw "God" was when we were coming home from church. Charlie was sitting in the back of the car when we passed a sculpture of the mythological figure Atlas, holding up the world. We passed it every day, but on that day for some reason, it made an impact on Charlie, who shouted, "There he is! There's God!"

If the Bible is to be believed, God smiles on that kind of faith and that kind of searching. Charlie's faith fed his imagination, and his imagination fed his faith. He was constantly searching for God and believed that God could do anything. It seems that children have a resiliency when it comes to faith and don't get as discouraged when God doesn't miraculously come through when or how they want. Their faith informs their belief that *God will act*.

They don't allow doubt or fear to be "the boss" of them.

From the beginning, David was special to God.

The first king of Israel was Saul, but he displeased God with his disobedience. Saul's servants believed that an evil spirit was tormenting the moody king. Since it was thought that a well-played harp could soothe and cure the tormented, the best harp player, a former shepherd boy named "David," entered Saul's service.

David was special indeed. His love of life and for God was contagious. David didn't know that there was something that he couldn't do. When he played his harp, the room grew quiet. The music was as beautiful as any had ever heard. David played for Saul again and again. And Saul found himself smiling. "I like him," he said to his servants. David played for Saul the next day and the next. And each day, Saul was getting better and thought, *The demons are leaving.* He whispered one day after David left, "I can finally breathe."

David soon became one of Saul's armor-bearers. Before long, Saul sent a messenger to David's father, Jesse, to ask if David, the youngest son, could remain in the king's service. "Allow David to stay in my service, for I am pleased with him," said Saul (1 Samuel 16:22).

☉ ☉ ☉

It happened that the Philistines, enemies of the Israelites, were gathering their forces for war. When Saul learned of the Philistines' advances, he assembled his army, and they camped in the Valley of Elah (1 Samuel 17:2). The Philistines were on one hill, and the Israelites were on another, with a valley between the two forces.

In the Philistine camp was a man named "Goliath." He was huge, over nine feet tall (1 Samuel 17:4), and he had been quite useful for the Philistines in battle. He was huge and capable. He wore a helmet and armor made of bronze. His spear was made of bronze and had an iron point (1 Samuel 17:4-7). Goliath was a scary sight.

One could suppose that Goliath had been able to lead the Philistines to victory on intimidation alone. Now that they were to battle the Israelites, the people whom supposedly God loved, Goliath was not about to be frightened. His victories had made him arrogant. And his lack of respect of God would reveal his ignorance.

"Why do you come out and line up for battle," he shouted to the Israelites. "Am I not a Philistine, and are you not the servants of Saul? Choose a man and have him come down to me. If he is able to fight and kill me, we will become your subjects; but if I overcome him and kill him, you will become our subjects and serve us" (1 Samuel 17:8-9).

Goliath's taunts were terrifying to the Israelite army and to Saul. There was no person and no army that could beat Goliath. He was too big and too strong. Nobody, including Saul, talked about God and how with God they could do all things. No, this wasn't a God-thing—not to them. This was flesh against flesh. And as far as they could tell, they were on the losing end.

Saul's army did not dare initiate a battle. They were too frightened. Twice a day, for forty days, Goliath came to within hearing distance of their camp and dared them to send one man out to fight him (1 Samuel 17:16). There need not be a lot of bloodshed, he reasoned. Just let there be a man-to-man duel. It would be settled, and both camps could go on their way.

For these forty days, young David continued attending to Saul, going back and forth from Saul to his father's sheep. He was too young for war. His father, though, was concerned for his other sons, who were encamped with the army. One day he told David to take food to them to see how they are doing (1 Samuel 17:17-19).

So, early the next morning, David left his father's house with the grain and bread, flour and cheeses, and headed toward the army encamped on the hill. As David approached the camp, he saw them leaving and heading toward their battle positions (1 Samuel 17:20). David heard his brothers talk of war and of their feats on the battlefield, but he had never been this close to the actual fighting. Excited, he dropped his parcel and got closer so that he could see and hear what was going on. It didn't occur to him to be afraid. He was only a child.

As he got closer, his eyes widened. Before him stood absolutely the biggest man he had ever seen. He had heard people talking about this giant. But David hadn't been able to imagine how big the giant really was. David thought, *He's huge!*

Goliath stood where he was and watched the Israelite army approach. He was surrounded by the Philistine army. When the Israelites got closer, the big man stepped away from his army and began issuing his usual taunts to the Israelites to send a man to fight. "This day, again, I defy the ranks of Israel!" Goliath thundered.

David's parents had always talked with him about God, who God was and what God could do. They had repeatedly told him that God was over all things and was to be respected. "You are to love the Lord your God with everything you've got," Jesse told his sons. David couldn't remember a day when his father hadn't reminded him of that duty, to love and serve God, and to have faith in God no matter what. David realized, listening to Goliath, that he was offended that this big man had the audacity to speak against the God he had been taught to love, honor, and respect.

The Israelite men repeated to David what the king had promised to the one man who killed the giant. But there was nobody able to do it, they told him. Nobody was big enough to kill the giant.

David found himself protesting in his spirit. He thought, *What about God? We've got God!* David asked more questions about the Philistine and why the men were so afraid. "Don't you believe in God?" he asked. They laughed at him because he was so young and naïve. Time and age would teach him.

David left the camp troubled, not only at what he had heard Goliath say but also at the Israelites' reaction. David thought, *What use is there in having a God if you don't believe? Is God good only when things are easy?*

When David got back to Saul, he shared what he had seen and heard. Saul nodded knowingly. He said that the situation was impossible. Even though he was king, Saul told the young boy, he didn't know what to do.

David couldn't understand, but inside his heart there was a burning anger against Goliath and a burning desire to show the giant who God was.

"I will go to fight the giant," he said to Saul.

Saul almost broke into laughter. Kids! They don't know anything, but they think that they know everything. How did little David think he was going to beat the giant? Kids don't think, they just believe. They have a faith that's almost stupid "crazy." It's the job of wise adults to save them.

As he looked at David, though, Saul saw something more than a child's idealism. He saw a love for God. It was as though the oil with which he had been anointed was now coming out of his pores, out of his eyes, spilling out of his heart. God clearly was with this child. But still Saul argued, "You are only a boy, and he has been fighting from his youth" (1 Samuel 17:33).

David declared, "Your servant has been keeping his father's sheep. When a lion or a bear came and carried off a sheep from the flock, I went after it, struck it, and rescued the sheep from its mouth. When it turned on me, I seized it by its hair, struck it, and killed it. Your servant has killed both the lion and the bear; this uncircumcised Philistine will be like one of them, because he has defied the armies of the living God. The LORD who delivered me from the paw of the lion and the paw of the bear will deliver me from the hand of this Philistine" (1 Samuel 17:34-37). In other words, "That giant is not the boss of me!"

Saul stood silent. He understood what was driving this child. "You can't say that you have faith if you're afraid," Jesse had told his sons. David had heard and seen the fear in the men of the army, and he had heard the defiance and disrespect of God in the giant's words. Saul knew that it was the God in David driving him to proclaim his faith and act on it.

Reluctantly, Saul said, "Go, and the LORD be with you." David started to run off, but Saul stopped him and told him that he'd have to go prepared, like a soldier. So David allowed himself to be dressed for battle. Saul put his tunic on the boy, then a coat of armor, and then a bronze helmet on his head. He was then given a sword, which he fastened on, and then he tried to walk around.

It was impossible. He was a boy used to running in the fields and over the hills. He felt like he had been stuffed into the garments. "I cannot go in these," he said to Saul, because I am not used to them." Saul protested, but David removed the garments and gear anyway. David grabbed his shepherd's staff and his sling, and then he started looking for stones. He chose five smooth stones from a stream and put them into his pouch. Then, with staff and sling in hand, he moved away from Saul and toward the Philistines (1 Samuel 17:39-40). Saul thought that David looked like a boy going off to play, not at all like a man equipped for battle. "Don't worry about me," David called back to Saul. "I am protected. God will protect me! God protected me from the lion and the bear; God will protect me from this brute, Goliath!" And he was gone.

When David got to the Israelites' camp, we may well imagine, he told the men that Saul had commissioned him to kill Goliath, and they roared with laughter. But David left them and headed toward the line of battle. As he approached, Goliath stood up. Here was a man coming to fight him. The contest was on! He roused his shield-bearer and told him that it was time, and the two of them headed toward the line of battle.

But when the two men—the little boy and the big giant—faced each other, Goliath grew angry. This was a child! Was this a ploy, a strategy, something to throw him off guard? He looked behind but saw nothing. Nor was there any movement in the camp. As he looked ahead, he could see the Israelite army standing off at a distance, watching.

Goliath looked down again at David. He was so young. He had no sword, no shield, nothing except a ridiculous sling. Goliath considered this a waste of his time. He was so angry and so loud. David listened as Goliath went on about how great he was and how the Israelites were punks, as was their God. "Who would send a little boy to fight in the place of men?" he bellowed. The more he talked, the angrier David became. "Come here," the giant gestured. "Come here, and I'll give your flesh to the birds of the air and to the beasts of the field" (1 Samuel 17:44).

David felt no fear, but rather a strange power. "You come against me with sword and spear and javelin, but I come against you in the name of the LORD Almighty, the God of the armies of Israel, whom you have defied," David said with boldness. "This day the LORD will hand you over to me, and I'll strike you down and cut off your head. Today I will give the carcasses of the Philistine army to the birds of the air and the beasts of the earth, and the whole world will know that there is a God in Israel. All those gathered here will know that it is not by sword or spear that the LORD saves; for the battle is the LORD's, and he will give all of you into our hands" (1 Samuel 17:45-47).

It was as if David said, "You are not the boss of me!"

The giant broke out into the loudest laughter that David had ever heard. But the laughter didn't distract him. As soon as he finished his proclamation, David ran toward Goliath, reaching into his pocket as he approached. Before Goliath could reach down and stop him, David had put a stone in his sling and aimed it at the giant's head. It hit Goliath dead center in the forehead. The giant touched his head, looked at his shield-bearer, tried to laugh again, and fell dead.

When the Philistines saw that Goliath was dead, they turned and ran away. The Israelites ran toward David and the dead giant.

Little David walked away. God was an awesome God, just as David's father had said.

Crazy-Faith Challenge

There are Goliaths all around us. We have to face them. Giants are everywhere, giants in the form of financial problems, inadequate health insurance, home foreclosures, mounting debt, failing marriages, and chronic depression. But what matters is the faith that we muster to tackle them. If we look at our giants independently, without God, they *are* Goliaths, huge and formidable. They make us cower and fear, as did the Israelite army. When the giants loom, we need God inside us, over us, and on each side. We, like David, need to feel like God is carrying us and is fighting the battle.

That kind of God-presence comes from seeking God, and the result of seeking God is that we find God. God with us, and God in us, gives us crazy faith, so that when the obstacles come, we can stare them in the face and say boldly, "You are not the boss of me!"

David noticed the men in the Israelite army worshiping their fear. David chose to worship the God of his father, and he faced his giant with crazy faith.

Something remarkable happens when our language complements our faith. Had David said, "He's too big," he could have been susceptible to fear, but by standing on his faith, he got bolder and stronger. He did not run, and he did not cower. He stood and faced his giant. There is a lesson in having that kind of faith, standing even when you are weak.

The bottom line: our problems are not the boss of us—God is. And when we know that and can proclaim it, crazy faith takes root.

chapter 6
waiting for deliverance

*I said, to the Lord, "I'm going to hold steady
on to you, and I know you'll see me through."*
—Harriet Tubman

It was crazy what Harriet Tubman set out to do.

Although she was called "Moses," when Tubman began her life's work of leading slaves to freedom, she was a young woman in her 20s and a fugitive slave—illiterate and penniless.

Working to free slaves on one occasion would have been crazy enough, but she made repeated trips into the Deep South, an estimated nineteen in all, resulting in the freeing of about three hundred slaves. Her work was hailed and appreciated, but few joined her risky mission. One biographer said that she was "cheered on by former fugitives but never joined by them on future expeditions."[1] She was spurred by her hatred of slavery, her love for her family, and her deep faith in God—a faith that truly could be called "crazy." She is said to have seen her faith as her only armor.[2]

The actual date of her birth is unknown, but it's thought that Tubman was born sometime between 1820 and 1822. Born to slave parents, Harriet Green and Ben Ross, she was named "Araminta Ross" and called "Minty." She didn't change her name to "Harriet" until she went north the first time. She received her last name, "Tubman," through her marriage to John Tubman, a free man. Her family lived on the Brodess plantation on the Eastern Shore of Maryland. By all accounts, they were a close family, which proved critical in Minty's future work as a liberator.

Araminta and her siblings grew up in slavery, being hired out to other plantations or working on the plantations of their parents. They had little, but they found joy in having each other.

Minty worked as a field hand for many of her young years, "following the oxen, loading and unloading wood, and carrying heavy burdens," which resulted in her gaining strength so noticeable that it "called forth the wonder of strong laboring men."[3] In retrospect, she viewed this time as God's way of preparing her for a life of hardship and endurance. She became a "marvelous specimen of physical womanhood, and before she was nineteen years old was a match for the strongest man on the plantation."[4]

It was her physical strength that helped her survive an incident that could have taken her life. She was in the presence of a slave who had left his plantation and gone to the village store for the evening. His overseer followed him and was furious. There are differing accounts, but the gist of the story is that the overseer wanted Araminta to help him whip his slave. Minty refused, and the slave started to run. As the slave moved toward the door, the overseer became frantic that the slave would get away and picked up a two-pound weight from a nearby counter and threw it at the slave. Instead, it struck Minty in her shawl-covered head. When the weight hit her, she reported, "it broke my skull and cut a piece of that shawl clean off and drove it into my head."[5] In her recollection of the incident years later, Tubman said her "hair had never been combed and it stood out like a bushel basket."[6] Her hair, she said, probably saved her life.

The injury disabled Tubman for life, and in the immediate time following the incident she became emaciated and weak, her flesh wasting away. Her owner wanted to sell her, but nobody wanted her. That was the labor pain for the birth of her crazy faith—a faith that would forever change her life and the lives of the people she led to freedom.

۞ ۞ ۞

From childhood, Tubman had always been religious. She always believed that God would deliver her and her family, and in any situation she always looked for the mercy and presence of God.

But following the injury, young Araminta experienced "an explosion of religious enthusiasm and vivid imagery."[7] She would report having visions and conversations with God and told the stories with such zeal that those around her had no doubt that God talked to her personally and had a plan that only she could know. Just as Moses had gone to the top of Mount Sinai and received the Ten Commandments, the injury that Harriet received at the hands of an angry overseer had been her Mount Sinai experience. And just as God had commanded Moses to become a conduit for the freedom of the Israelites, so had God commissioned Araminta Ross—Harriet Tubman—to be the Moses of her people.

Friends and family of Tubman likewise grew to trust and depend on her faith, the likes of which nobody else at that time seemed to have: "I never met with any person of any color who had more confidence in the voice of God, as spoken direct to her soul," said one associate.[8] Another person who knew Tubman said, "She could elude patrols and pursuers with as much ease and unconcern as an eagle would soar through the heavens." She "had faith in God," always asking God to direct her and show her what to do, and God always did. She would talk about "consulting with God" just like someone would consult a friend on business matters.[9]

Tubman's crazy faith was evidenced in some of the actions that she took. Her efforts to lead her people to freedom always were in need of financing. She led groups of people north in the winter. In the spring and summer months, she worked as a domestic or at other odd jobs in order to make the trip again. She led the slaves to freedom, but she also took care of them. And she needed money to do that.

She had supporters who helped her: abolitionists, Quakers, and people who were just generally opposed to slavery and resentful that the Fugitive Slave Act made it mandatory for found fugitive slaves to be returned to their masters.

God was the real conductor on Tubman's underground railroad. And while Tubman never made any bones about her beliefs, she had great fears about what God told her to do. After she had secured her own freedom and then gone back twice for family members from the North into the South, she was clear that God was telling her to lead more of her people from slavery to freedom. It was a crazy assignment—and a dangerous one.

But she also remained sure that God was in control. Expressing her fears to God, she said, "The Lord told me to do this. I said, 'Oh Lord, I can't—don't ask me—take somebody else.'" But she also said that in reply to her protestations, God said directly to her, "It's you I want, Harriet Tubman."[10]

Her absolute faith that God had charged her with a peculiar and particular mission was driven home the moment she crossed into freedom herself in 1849. "I was *free*, but there was no one to welcome me to the land of freedom," Tubman said. "I was a stranger in a strange land; and my home, after all, was down in Maryland; because my father, my mothers, my brothers, my sisters and friends were there. But I was free, and *they* should be free. I would make a home in the North and bring them there, God helping me. Oh, how I prayed then....I said, to the Lord, 'I'm going to hold steady on to *you*, and I *know* you'll see me through.'"[11]

From that point, Tubman saw her life as being irreversibly intertwined with the will of God. God could not be pleased with what was happening; God surely wanted the slaves to be free just like God had wanted the Israelites to be free. Tubman was sure that she was hearing God rightly, and since it was God's will, she believed that she would be safe and that God's work and will would be done. It has to be assumed that as this illiterate black woman went back and forth from freedom to hostile slave territory, with the authorities looking for her and any other escaping slave, she had bouts of real fear. But crazy faith gave her what she needed. She began to look on the events of her childhood as preparation for what she had been sent to do on this earth. Because she could not read or write, we are not privy to the "down" moments that she must have had in her work, but clearly her faith in God lifted her and enabled her to empower other people to seek their freedom. That is crazy faith at its best.

When we hear of Harriet Tubman and the Underground Railroad, it's as if the experience happened on paper and not in real life. We are unable to taste, see, and feel the drama, danger, and discomfort that the slaves endured, and how Tubman used her faith to see them through.

There was always the financial burden. Tubman constantly worked to get money for the freedom project, never letting the slaves know who would be freed and how critical a job that was. Part of Tubman's job was to keep the slaves' heads above the waters of fear and doubt. A fearful slave would never be able go get through the wilderness. And a wilderness it was. The escaping slaves never traveled by day, but rather always at night, guided by Tubman and her reliance on the North Star. They normally traveled in the winter because "that's the time most people are in their houses," Tubman said. More people in their houses meant fewer people on their trails.

There were times when slaves arrived at their destinations suffering severe frostbite because they had traveled roads in the dead of winter with no shoes. They sometimes reached their freedom sick with pneumonia or some other respiratory disease because they had been forced to lie in a swampy marsh at night while bounty hunters passed.

On her last trip to Maryland, she and the slaves ran dangerously close to being captured. Tubman "received a telegraph from her unseen Protector" and quickly changed course. The change resulted in all of them being stuck in a swamp, "where the grass grew tall and rank, and where no human being could be suspected of seeking a hiding place."[12] It was to this God-forsaken place that Harriet guided her group, demanding that they not complain or say a word. The babies who were with them were drugged to keep them quiet.

For some time they lay there, quiet, tired, sick, wet, and hungry, "waiting for deliverance." Tubman says that although her group was in wretched condition, she dared not leave them to get provisions, because she was sure that a man at whose door she had knocked earlier "had given the alarm in town, and officers might be on watch for them."[13] But Tubman's "faith never wavered, her silent prayer ascended, and she confidently expected help from some quarter or other."[14]

When night fell, a Quaker passed by the group, saying out loud, but never stopping as he spoke, that there was a horse and a wagon in a designated place. Tubman heard it and claimed it as her answer from God. When she was sure that the coast was clear, Tubman led her haggard, sick, cold, and hungry group to the place of which the Quaker had spoken. Sure enough, there was the horse and wagon. Tubman never understood how the mysterious man knew of their presence, but she attributed it to her God and her prayer, which "was the prayer of faith, and she *expected* an answer."[15]

Personal experiences also served as potential hindrances to Tubman's mission. Her own husband, John Tubman, a free man, was not at all interested in the freedom movement and did not support or believe in her efforts at freeing the slaves. Tubman had no way of knowing how deeply his doubt and lack of support would affect her, until she returned home after having been gone for two years and having freed a number of slaves by then. When she got home from her third trip, she found that her husband had married another woman. She was crushed. Surely God hadn't allowed this to happen. She loved her husband and had looked forward to them living together in freedom. His infidelity almost crushed Tubman's spirit, but then her crazy faith kicked in and gave her a new determination. What humans meant for evil, God meant for good. By example, Tubman showed her charges how to handle adversity—physical, emotional, and spiritual.

Tubman's story is such a rich one. Her life was not just about going back and forth freeing slaves; it was also about working in the Civil War and working for women's rights. None of what she did was easy, but all of what she did was done with the absolute belief that the impossible could be done because of God.

She did not end her life as a wealthy woman, though she was well-known and highly respected. Crazy faith does not necessarily make you rich monetarily. But crazy faith does produce change in the world.

In thinking about crazy faith and what Tubman did for her people, we can go back to the Bible for a moment to the story of the feeding of the five thousand found in the Gospel of John (John 6:1-15). In this story, Jesus and his disciples had gone off by themselves, but a huge crowd followed because of the healings that he had done. There were at least five thousand men, plus an untold number of women and children.

After Jesus had been teaching for a while, he turned to his disciples, specifically Andrew and Philip. To Philip he said, "Where shall we buy bread for these people to eat?" Philip, looking at the huge number of people before him, seemed bothered and said, "Eight months' wages would not buy enough bread for each one to have a bite!" (John 6:5, 7).

Then Andrew brought to Jesus a young boy who had two fish and five loaves of barley bread. The fish probably were like sardines, packed together and pickled, and barley bread was the staple of poor people. Nevertheless, Andrew, facing this large number of hungry people, had the audacity to say to Jesus, "Here is a boy with five small barley loaves and two small fish" (John 6:9).

Then Andrew asked, "But how will they feed so many?" And it's striking that he found a small boy who had five small barley loaves and five small fish.

Small—the size of beginning faith.

Crazy-Faith Challenge

How impossible is it to feed over five thousand people with such a small quantity? How significant is a small, unknown boy for such a big task?

It is the seeing or believing in the absolutely impossible, the birth of something truly big from something incredibly small, that makes for crazy faith. It is faith that moves mountains. It is faith that changes the world. Feeding a multitude with a small ration of food and a pot full of faith or leading slaves to freedom armed only with a dream guided by the North Star—that certainly is crazy faith. Harriet Tubman had it. Jesus truly had it. Do you? How strong is your faith?

chapter 7
questions, trumpets, and jars

The LORD is with you, mighty warrior.
—Judges 6:12, NRSV

We are taught not to question God. We've been told that questioning God is equal to the ultimate disrespect. God is omnipotent, and so God knows best. So if we are true believers, we are taught not to question. We simply accept what God says and does.

There are at least two problems with that view. One is that it actually hampers faith. There are things that we simply do not understand, and so we need to have the freedom to question. Having faith implies and requires that we have a relationship with God, and no relationship is possible without questions. Sure, some of the biblical heroes did as God asked without questioning. But we don't have to look far in the text to find others who did question God, and quite vehemently so.

That leads to the second problem: not questioning God is actually unbiblical. We know that as Job suffered, he asked questions of God, and one finds scores of questions being asked of God by David in the Psalms. Yes, David praises and thanks God, but he also questions God. And Jesus himself questions God, quoting Psalm 22:1 as he dies on the cross. In Psalm 10 the writer asks, "Why, O LORD, do you stand far off? Why do you hide yourself in times of trouble?" (Psalm 10:1). The writer in Psalm 13 asks,

"How long, O LORD? Will you forget me forever? How long will you hide your face from me? How long must I wrestle with my thoughts and every day have sorrow in my heart? How long will my enemy triumph over me?" (Psalm 13:1-2).

Things happen on the walk of faith that aren't understandable. Knowing that we have a God who allows questions actually strengthens our relationship with God. We have the assurance that God does not require us to be superhuman and endure suffering or circumstances as if we are not struggling. Asking God questions allows us to know God better by reminding us of all that has been done for us, and those things strengthen us for the moment at hand. So in asking questions we grow closer to God, and asking questions is a legitimate part of prayer. What must accompany the questions, though, is a time of silence to hear God's response.

So is it all right to doubt what God has told us to do? Absolutely, for the ways of God are not our ways! The things that God sees for us we cannot begin to see for ourselves.

One of my deacons became ill with a brain tumor, and one of her sons was in great distress after her surgery. "Can I ask why?" he said. "She's my mother. She's such a good person. Can I ask why?" I told him yes, ask. We exist to do God's work and will, but God exists to give us hope, joy, peace, direction—and faith. This young man asked God why, and later he told me that God never gave him an answer to the question, but God had given him peace.

Questioning God doesn't lead us to hell; it gives birth to crazy faith.

◉ ◉ ◉

The story of Gideon is familiar to many of us not because it tells of his faith and conviction, but rather because it shows how someone questions God and insists on signs to prove that God is telling him to do the impossible.

The Israelites, according to Judges, "did evil in the eyes of the LORD, and for seven years he gave them into the hands of the Midianites" (Judges 6:1). The Israelites' oppression at the hands of the Midianites was so bad that they built hiding places in caves and on mountain clefts. They were not safe anywhere, and whenever they had success in planting crops, the Midianites and the Amalekites plundered and invaded their land (Judges 6:2-3). The enemies of the Israelites killed their cattle and ruined their land "all the way to Gaza." It was said that when invasions came, they came suddenly and swiftly, and the Midianites "swarmed on them like locusts; there were so many of them that it was impossible to count them" (Judges 6:5-6). The Israelites were impoverished and afraid. They finally called out to the Lord for help.

When they called to God, it was an angry God who answered. God reminded them of all that had already been done for them, rescuing them from slavery in Egypt, bringing them through the wilderness, giving them the land in the faces of their enemies. God reminded them that all that was asked of them in return was loyalty. "I said to you, 'I am the LORD your God; do not worship the gods of the Amorites, in whose land you live.' But you have not listened to me" (Judges 6:10).

The Israelites were known to stray away from God and God's desires. They were quick to forget God's goodness and worship the gods of their oppressors. Whatever the reason, the Israelites had been known to wander from God, and every time they did, God fumed. This time was no exception.

God, in the presence of an angel, appeared to Gideon, coming under the oak in Ophrah that belonged to his father, Joash the Abiezrite. Gideon was under the tree, threshing wheat in a winepress to keep it from the Midianites. The angel watched Gideon for a while and then said to him, "The LORD is with you, mighty warrior" (Judges 6:11-12).

Gideon didn't stop what he was doing. He heard the angel's proclamation, but he scoffed. *With us, indeed!* Gideon thought. It was a stupid thing to say to a man who was leading people who hadn't won a single battle in years. He wasn't about to curse God, but he wasn't about to praise God either.

When Gideon spoke back to the angel, his voice showed irritation. "But sir," Gideon replied, "if the LORD is with us, why has all this happened to us? Where are all his wonders that our fathers told us about when they said, 'Did not the LORD bring us up out of Egypt?' But now the LORD has abandoned us and put us into the hand of Midian" (Judges 6:13).

God must have fumed: *How quickly you humans forget. When it's convenient to remember what I've done, you're all into your history, but as soon as you get comfortable, you choose to forget me and what I've done. You remember only when you're in danger or when you're hurting.* Then the LORD said to Gideon, "Go in the strength you have and save Israel out of Midian's hand. Am I not sending you?" (Judges 6:14).

Gideon had a problem with God's request. Gideon no longer believed in himself after losing so many battles, so why would God want to use *him* to save Israel? It was a crazy request. And Gideon voiced his objections. "But Lord, how can I save Israel?" he asked. "My clan is the weakest in Manasseh, and I am the least in my family" (Judges 6:15, NIV). The angel reminded Gideon that God would be with him. God was sending him, so surely God would not abandon him.

But Gideon was not so quick to take God's word. He wasn't even sure it was God who was really speaking to him. Still, Gideon didn't want to dismiss this angel if it really was a herald of God. So, he decided to find out if and what God was really requiring of him. "If now I have found favor in your eyes, give me a sign that it is really you talking to me. Please do not go away until I come back and bring my offering and set it before you" (Judges 6:17-18).

And God consented to wait.

When Gideon offered the sacrifice, the angel of God gave him some instructions. "Take the meat and the unleavened bread, place them on this rock, and pour out the broth," the angel said. When Gideon did as he was asked, "the angel of the LORD touched the meat and the unleavened bread. Fire flared from the rock, consuming the meat and bread" (Judges 6:20-21).

Whoa! God had been made known. And although Gideon was happy at the sign, he was also frightened. How could he have demanded God to give him a sign?

"Peace!" God said to Gideon. "Do not be afraid. You are not going to die" (Judges 6:23).

Gideon was relieved, but just to make sure that God understood his intentions, he built an altar to God at that place and called it "The LORD is Peace" (Judges 6:24).

Gideon had not forgotten that God had asked him to move against the Midianites, and God had not forgotten that Gideon needed signs to convince him to be obedient. It was a crazy thing that God was asking Gideon to do. What Gideon knew for sure was that God had been on that rock and consumed the meat and unleavened bread.

The Midianites, the Amalekites, and the other enemies of the Israelites were joining forces. The Israelites were so tired of being beaten, so tired of being oppressed. They had called on God the last time, and God hadn't saved them, so they had no faith that God would respond. But Gideon took a trumpet and summoned the Abiezrites to follow him. As Gideon gathered the men, he wondered what he was doing. They had no weapons and no supplies, and they were tired. But he continued to call forth men for battle, men from the tribes of Napthali, Asher, and Zebulun. To his surprise, they answered the call (Judges 6:33-35).

Only God, Gideon thought.

Night had fallen as the last of the men gathered, giving Gideon time to talk with God. He absolutely did not know what to do next. And so covered by the protection of night, he talked to God. "If you will save Israel by my hand as you have promised—look, I will place a wool fleece on the threshing floor. If there is dew only on the fleece and all the ground is dry, then I will know that you will save Israel by my hand, as you have said" (Judges 6:36-37). Gideon placed the wool fleece on the floor, careful to make sure that there was not a drop of dampness on it. Several times during the night he awakened and touched the fleece and found that it was still completely dry. He finally fell into a deep sleep and did not awaken until morning. When he arose, he touched the fleece, and it dripped with morning's heavy dew. He was able to squeeze a bowlful of water (Judges 6:38).

It was good. As he looked at the bowl of water, he talked with God again. "Do not be angry with me. Let me make just one more request," Gideon said. "Allow me one more test with the fleece. This time make the fleece dry and the ground covered with dew" (Judges 6:39). God obliged, for God needed for people to know that he was God, starting with Gideon. In the morning, when Gideon awoke, the fleece was bone dry, and the ground was saturated with the morning's dew.

It was crazy-faith time, and it was also time for divine battle.

As Gideon walked toward his men, he knew that God was with him, and that God was in this thing that was about to happen. He didn't know how many Midianites there were, but he was sure that there were upward of three hundred thousand. Gideon looked at his men. He surmised that he had over thirty thousand men. That wasn't a lot of men, but if it was God's intent to win this battle, Gideon could do it.

As Gideon moved toward the troops, he heard God's voice: "You have too many men for me to deliver Midian into their hands. In order that Israel may not boast against me that her own strength has saved her, announce now to the people, 'Anyone who trembles with fear may turn back and leave Mount Gilead'" (Judges 7:2-3). Gideon's knees nearly buckled as twenty-two thousand men left (Judges 7:4).

There were ten thousand men left against three hundred thousand, maybe four hundred thousand, of the enemy. *It was impossible*, Gideon must have thought. *Surely, God had a plan. Surely, God was in this.*

Then God spoke again: "There are still too many men. Take them down to the water, and I will sift them for you there. If I say, 'This one shall go with you,' he shall go; but if I say, 'This one shall not go with you,' he shall not go" (Judges 7:4).

God knew that Gideon was worried, but God appreciated that he was trying to hold on and give the appearance of having faith—a crazy faith. Only one who truly loved him would do this.

When the then thousand men got to the water, they were told to drink, and God told Gideon to separate those who lapped the water with their tongues like dogs from the ones who knelt down to drink (Judges 7:5-6). Gideon did as he was told. When the separation was complete, God said, "With the three hundred men that lapped I will save you and give the Midianites into your hands" (Judges 7:7).

As 9,700 men left, Gideon held his head in his hands. How would they pull this off? As the men left and gave their food and trumpets to the three hundred, Gideon had to shake his head. "We have nothing. Nothing! We have trumpets and three hundred men. How in the world are we going to do this?" This was crazier than the Red Sea parting and making it through forty years in the wilderness. Everyone knew that to fight effectively, one had to have men and weapons.

That night, sensing Gideon's apprehension, God woke his young warrior and told him to take a servant and approach the camp of the Midianites. There, God promised, Gideon would hear something that would encourage him. So Gideon took his servant Purah, and the two men approached the Midianite camp.

Everywhere Gideon looked he saw Midianites and people ready to destroy the Israelites. There were so many that they looked like the fields when they were covered with locusts. Not only were they numerous, but also they had weapons. They had strategically set themselves around the Israelites, who therefore had no way to escape. As they settled in around their campfires, they could be heard laughing, a laughter that bespoke confidence of the impending battle. They ate well and drank hard.

Gideon arrived where God had directed him in time to hear a conversation between two of his enemies. "I had a dream," one man said. "A round loaf of barley bread came tumbling into the Midianite camp. It struck the tent with such force that the tent overturned and collapsed" (Judges 7:13).

Gideon wasn't impressed with the dream, and he wondered why God had him stop there. It seemed like a waste of time. But his whole body stiffened as he heard the response of the man's friend: "This can be nothing other than the sword of Gideon son of Joash, the Israelite. God has given the Midianites and the whole camp into his hands" (Judges 7:14).

Out of all the conversations that he could have heard, Gideon was allowed by God to hear this one. These two men knew Gideon's name and his father's name. And they heard that Gideon was leading a battle, but the true commander was God. How had they known that? True, enemies throughout Israel's history had known about God, and how God fought the battles. But it had been seven years of steady defeat for the Israelites. Gideon thought that the enemy believed that God had forsaken the Israelites, and that's why the time for battle was so ripe.

Perhaps so, but the words of these men didn't communicate that. How could a round loaf of bread knock a whole tent down? Gideon found himself encouraged, just as God had promised. All God wanted Gideon to do was believe in God's greatness, situation and circumstances notwithstanding. God wanted Gideon to communicate to his men that God was capable of the most impossible things in the most impossible situations. Whatever weapon Gideon had, it would act as a sword and bring victory to God.

Gideon got it.

He and the servant rushed back to the camp. "Get up!" he said to them. "The LORD has given the Midianite camp into your hands" (Judges 7:15). Stunned out of their sleep, the men began to ask for weapons. Gideon heard but ignored them, and under God's direction he divided the men into three groups of one hundred each. All of the men were then given trumpets and empty jars with torches (Judges 7:16).

There was a pause. Um, they were going to *battle*. What in the world would they do with trumpets and empty jars?

But Gideon didn't dare try to explain. "Watch me," he said. "Follow my lead. When I get to the edge of the camp, do exactly as I do. When I and all who are with me blow our trumpets, then from all around the camp, blow yours too and shout, 'For the LORD and for Gideon'" (Judges 7:17-18).

Absolutely crazy. Gideon knew it as well as the men did. He and his one hundred men approached the camp, and the other two hundred stood where they were directed. Just as the guards of the Midianite camp were changing, Gideon and his one hundred men blew their trumpets and smashed the jars that were in their hands. It was awful, and it was loud. The Midianites were stunned and frightened. "A sword for the LORD and a sword for Gideon!" Gideon's men shouted (Judges 7:20). The Midianites didn't know what to make of the situation and were terrified.

The more Gideon and his men saw terror on the faces of the Midianites, the louder they blew the trumpets.

While Gideon and his men carried out their battle plan, God caused the Midianites to become confused, and they turned on each other with their swords. Gideon could hear some of them babbling as they fought, but he couldn't make out what they were saying. The Midianites were dying, as was their threat to decimate the Israelites. After seven long years of heartache and hard times, it was over. God was delivering the Israelites.

Crazy-Faith Challenge

Gideon wept as he realized what God had done in spite of Gideon's own doubts. God had used three hundred men, trumpets, and empty jars. God smiled even as Gideon wept, because Gideon had seen that crazy faith works. Gideon saw that when God is honored, God honors in return. The biblical story is detailed, but the lesson is simple. It takes faith to follow God. We go into battle every day armed with what we have—our hopes and dreams, our failures and our successes. That's all we have, but it's what God gave us and equipped us with for the struggles ahead. We just have to believe. It takes a mighty faith to believe that God will do the impossible if we simply trust and obey—and commit to God's directive even when it seems downright ridiculous.

chapter 8
where to go, not how to get there

*There are poor people in the world because
you and I do not share enough.*
—Mother Teresa

There is something disconcerting about poverty. It is disconcerting
to see it and even more troubling to touch it or experience it.

On my first trip to West Africa, I was disturbed by the stench
from the open gutters, the lack of paved streets and sidewalks, and
the absence of skyscrapers. When I've traveled to Caribbean
islands or to Mexico, I have been struck by the disparity between
the posh tourist retreats and the shabby living spaces of those who
provide the travelers with comfort. I was appalled by the squalor
I saw among the indigenous people in Cancun and in Jamaica.

In South Africa, the material poverty in the townships really
bothered me. These townships were close to the opulence of
Capetown, where I was staying. I say "material poverty" because
the people there were not poor in spirit. The children greeted us
with joy and enthusiasm, as did the children in West Africa. They
were so content to be given the smallest gift, but the living conditions were horrid by most Western standards.

In the United States, the poverty in spite of this nation's wealth is
even more disconcerting. When I was a reporter, I remember visiting a house where an invalid woman lived with her grandchildren.

The ceiling was broken, and one could see the bottom floor from the second floor. Roaches were everywhere, and I was sickened. They were in the refrigerator, in the stove, in the sink, and crawling all over the dog's bowl filled with food.

In another house I visited one winter, there was one room where a family of seven huddled so that they wouldn't freeze. The whole family was barely warmed by the heat that came from the oven. It was so cold, even with the oven on. I shivered as I talked with them.

I visited another woman who was sick but too poor to afford health care. When I saw her, she was lying in her own vomit. She was too weak to move. Her house was drafty, and the stench was sickening. I felt such a sense of helplessness visiting these families because I didn't know what I could do.

But Mother Teresa saw poverty, and listening to God, she realized not only that she *could* do something, but *must* do something. Her life became an example of crazy faith working. She was obedient to God's command to her to serve "the poorest of the poor." Mother Teresa's faith moved her to obey God. Her faith made it possible for millions of poor people to be helped and rich people to be moved to help.

☉ ☉ ☉

She was born in Skopje (capital of what is now the Republic of Macedonia), on August 26, 1910, to Nicholas and Drana Bojaxhiu, and christened with the name "Agnes." When Agnes was twelve, she began to feel the pull of God on her life. She was especially moved by the reports of Jesuit priests who were doing missionary work in Bengal, India. She felt a stirring in her soul that said that her work would be in India as well.

When she grew older, Agnes shared her call with her parish priest and asked how she could be sure that God was calling her, and calling her to do what she believed she'd heard.

"You will know it by your inner happiness," he said. "If you feel happy with the idea that God is calling you in order that you serve him and your neighbor, that's the best proof of your vocation."[1]

Happiness might not have been her emotion, but she was content and sure of what she had heard from God. Agnes applied to the Loreto order, located in Bengal. She was instructed to go to Ireland, where she would learn English, and from there her course would be charted. So, at age eighteen she boarded a train and left her family in Skopje.

It was the beginning of her crazy-faith walk for God.

But she did not begin the work to which God had called her—serving the poorest of the poor. After spending two months in Ireland, she was sent to a convent in Darjeeling, India, where she studied for two years as a novice. She stayed a few days in Calcutta on her way to Darjeeling, and the contrast between the two places made an indelible imprint on her being. Darjeeling was a beautiful city, quiet and scenic, while Calcutta was a bustling city, where the lives of the very rich and very poor stood side by side in stark contrast. In Calcutta, the young girl was able to see human misery in ways she had never before seen, but she was there for less than a week. She had to go to Darjeeling to receive instruction for her life as a nun.

She took her vows in 1931—the three vows of poverty, chastity, and obedience—and became officially a sister of Loreto[2] and adopted the name "Teresa." She began teaching at St. Mary's High School, located in Entally, a suburb of Calcutta. She remained there for seventeen years, first as a teacher and later as principal.[3] Ironically, given the nature of her life's work, Sister Teresa worked in the high school that was for the city's more affluent girls. There was another high school, in the same vicinity, for girls who could not afford the tuition. Sister Teresa loved being in Calcutta and teaching at St. Mary's High School, and she shared her joy with her mother in a letter, but her mother reminded her, "Never forget that the only reason for your going forth to a country so far away was the poor."[4]

Her mother's words must have jostled her spiritual senses. On the way to Darjeeling for a spiritual retreat, she recounts that she went through something of a vocational crisis and a deepening of her faith.[5] She realized that God was calling her to "serve the poorest of the poor," and she would be required to leave the convent in Entally. The thought grieved her, for she had been there much of her young life. But on the train, God spoke to her clearly and told her that she was not only to serve the poor, but also to *live among the poor*. The directive was clear, though she didn't know how it could ever come to be. To live among the poor meant that she would have to leave the convent. As far as she knew, nobody had ever done that.

Think about what this thirty-eight-year-old woman was doing. It is one thing to work "with the poor," to "go out" and do some charitable things and then go back to a warm home with food, heat, and lights and all the comforts that we crave. But that's not what Mother Teresa did. She understood God to be telling her to *live among the poor*. She understood God to be saying that she had to experience life through their eyes, and it was to this command that she said yes.

But can you picture it? Think of driving through the "bad areas" of your town and praying that your car won't break down. Think of the fear that you've felt, or maybe the disgust, as you walked past a person begging on the street. Have you ever avoided the eyes of the people that you saw on the street because you were either afraid or turned off or just didn't know what to do? Have you ever seen a person who appeared to be ill, and you, out of fear, left that person alone and didn't seek help? Have you ever smelled the stench and been nauseated as someone used the street as a toilet? Have you ever seen a pile of old clothing or blankets on the sidewalk, and, to your surprise, realized there was a person under it?

It was into that type of environment that Mother Teresa went, away from the warmth and comfort of the convent in which she had lived for twenty years.

From the moment she left the convent and hit the streets of Calcutta, the only weapon that she had was her faith. The sounds of the suffering seemed to explode in her ears. Everywhere she looked, there were suffering poor people. She saw people so close to death that they were hardly breathing. There were naked children, sitting quietly on the streets, their eyes wide with pain and miserable in their own bodies. She saw people who had lost legs pulling themselves along on the streets on their hands, begging for just a few rupees so that they might eat. Every once in a while, she'd hear an agonized scream of one of these people, and it startled her but bothered her more. These were God's children, the souls for whom Jesus died. They needed to know that God loved them. God was telling her that she should help *these* people.

Sister Teresa had virtually nothing in terms of material possessions, and she wanted none. These people had nothing either. She had to *be* one of them in order to be able to do what God was telling her to do. As she began her work with the poor in earnest, she knew that she would have to depend on God for everything, and she had to *know* that God was with her and that God would provide. That's called crazy faith.

"To serve the poorest of the poor" became her fourth vow. The call of Christ would be answered not just by service to the poor, but through love given to the poor. God revealed to Sister Teresa on the train that people were thirsty for God, and God wanted to satisfy that thirst. It wasn't just their poverty in terms of money that was killing them; it was their poverty of love. They had nobody to touch them, to share with them, to listen to them or take them seriously. They were allowed to die on the streets and then virtually were thrown away. *These are God's children*, Mother Teresa thought. In her mind, every person born was special because he or she belonged to God. And no matter how poor or sick one was, one still needed to know the power of God's love. Her work was to be done among those who had been abandoned, who had nobody; her ministry was to show them that they had God.[6]

Living among the poor allowed her to see their pain through their eyes and to feel what they felt daily. She found herself praying that God's love in her would never run dry, because these people needed it so much. As young women vied to work with her, she would explain to them that this ministry was no picnic; it was hard, heartbreaking work, but so necessary. "In order to understand poverty," she would tell them, "you have to touch it."[7]

From the beginning, because she was being sent into this wilderness with nothing, she had to depend totally on God. She would learn and would teach those who wanted to become engaged in the work three words that they must never forget: *dependence, detachment, dedication.*[8] She would learn those three words in her early years, beginning with a faith that demanded complete dependence on God. That kind of dependence required one to detach oneself from the world and from the material comforts that the world offered and be dedicated to the work at hand. It would be impossible, she said, to do the work without living those three principles. The poor, she believed, were forcibly detached from the comforts of the world due to their conditions. If she was going to truly minister to them, be like them, live with them, and understand them, she could not look mournfully back to what she was missing but instead must grasp hold of the benefits of loving and depending completely on God.

Doing so, she taught, would provide the "happiness" that her parish priest had spoken of so long ago when she had first verbalized what her call was to be.

◎ ◎ ◎

It might have been the sight of so many people dying on the streets of Calcutta that bothered her most. Mother Teresa saw them as abandoned by Christians. Early in her work with the poor she came across a woman "half-eaten by rats, lying in the rain on the sidewalk, ignored by passersby and dying. After carrying the woman to several nearby hospitals, where she was repeatedly refused admission, Mother Teresa watched the woman die in her arms."[9]

It was almost more than she could take. She was emotionally traumatized by the realization that people would treat suffering animals better than they would treat suffering fellow human beings. As she looked around, she could see and hear on the streets of Calcutta God's children, suffering. As she looked at them, she saw Jesus and was reminded of the Scripture that said, "Inasmuch as ye have done it unto one of the least of these…, ye have done it to me" (Matthew 25:40, KJV). Part of her call, she realized, was to teach people, religious people who said that they knew God, that each person suffering belonged to God and was special to God. To ignore them was to ignore God! One could not say that one belonged to God or loved God and yet let those people suffer as they did.

Following her experience with the dying woman, and moved by her faith and her total dependence on God, she went to the mayor of Calcutta and expressed her concern for the people dying on the streets. She asked the mayor for a place where she could take care of the dying people of Calcutta.[10]

The mayor offered her a choice of two locations; she declined to take a place in a nicer part of the city, because it was in an area "rarely visited by the poor."[11] Instead, she chose a dirty, dilapidated structure in an area riddled with crime. It was actually a *dormashalah*, a place of free lodging for people from outside of Calcutta who came to visit the goddess Kali, the protector goddess of the city.[12]

This rundown place became what is today known as Nirmal Hriday. From the beginning, it was a place for anyone who was dying and who had been abandoned, whether Christian or Hindu. Mother Teresa's goal was to provide the dying with dignity. Her crazy faith made her believe that such a goal could be accomplished in a place where, up to that point, nobody had cared one iota for the thousands of people who languished on the streets.

The more Mother Teresa worked with the poor, the more intense became her passion for them. She taught that the Sisters of Charity, which is what those who worked with her in her new order were called, were "not to wear gloves to touch the maggot-ridden bodies of the dying, any more than they were to hold lepers at arm's length, because they were tending the body of Christ."[13] The abandonment of people with leprosy got to her, and so she and the Sisters of Charity began to seek them out.

Mother Teresa's faith spilled over onto the young women (and, eventually, men as well) who wanted to work with her. Stones were thrown at them sometimes as they carried dying people into Nirmal Hriday to "die beautifully." People watched with horror and disgust as the sisters applied soothing ointments to dying, maggot-infested bodies and watched as Mother Teresa was on her hands and knees scrubbing the floors. Everyone was a child of God, she would say. She made no distinction between faiths or gender; no illness was too awful, no death too hideous for her to ignore. To ignore anyone was to ignore the Christ. She believed that if she took care of God's children, God would take care of her.

Miracles happened. There were times when it seemed that all was lost, but Mother Teresa, who prayed continually and demanded that every Sister of Charity do the same, would say to them, "I want you to have complete confidence that God won't let us down. Take him at his word and seek first the kingdom of heaven, and all else will be added on. Joy, peace, and unity are more important than money."[14] She had learned of God's faithfulness through her experiences, and she never lost a moment to share the lessons of faith that had been deeply ingrained in her spirit. She had learned that crazy faith "feeds" God. She would not have phrased it that way, but it seems that God was in fact fed by her faith.

For Mother Teresa, the biggest miracles were those in which people, children of God, who had formerly been discarded and abandoned now got glimpses of God's love. To her, it was the transforming power of God's love. She once said, "There are poor people in the world because you and I do not share enough."[15] It was the poverty of the spirit that was doing the most damage, and it was the mission of the Sisters of Charity, living with the "poorest of the poor," to bring a unique wealth to those situations.

Mother Teresa had faith of biblical proportions—not unlike that of Moses, who watched the Red Sea part; or little David, who killed the giant Goliath with a stone and a sling; or the woman who believed the prophet Elisha when he told her to gather oil when there was none, and who ended up getting enough oil to pay her debts and still have oil left over.

Mother Teresa boldly asserted that her God, this God who was with her in the streets and now all over the world, could do anything. She was a woman who believed in prayer and who went off by herself several times a day to pray.

A devout Roman Catholic and strict adherent to its tenets, she ministered to anyone and everyone who had been abandoned or was sick, dying, or alone. She taught her Sisters of Charity to do the same. It was quite a strange sight to see this Roman Catholic nun tending to Hindus and Muslims. Dr. Zakir Husain, a Muslim and the president of India from 1967 to 1969, recalled the time when Hindus, afraid and threatened by Mother Teresa as they watched her pick up sick and dying children off the streets of

Calcutta, were humbled when they realized that the children they had thrown out were the very ones Mother Teresa was taking in. To her, all humans were children of God and therefore precious. He called her a saint. Mother Teresa merely chose to say that faith is shown in actions, and she showed by her actions that faith and love are not denominational in nature.[16]

She believed that much of the suffering of the world was due to the fact that people don't share enough, and she also believed that human beings had the capacity to care for the poorest of the poor if they just saw an example.

From one woman and her faith and love was born a worldwide movement to help the poor. "By 1990, 456 centers to treat the poor had been established in 100 countries. In 1990 alone, 500,000 families were fed, 20,000 slum children were taught in 124 schools, 90,000 leprosy patients were treated, and over 17,000 'shut-ins' had been visited,"[17] says Navin Chawla.

With her crazy faith, Mother Teresa touched the poorest of the poor and impacted the world in a way that one would never have expected one woman to do.

Crazy-Faith Challenge

Many times we feel inspired or think that we hear God telling us to do something that is completely beyond the scope of our imagination. How many times have we thought a great thought or heard what we thought was the voice of God telling us to go to a place, dream a dream, or embark on a project, but we are so overwhelmed by the thought that we simply do not move forward? Maybe it's time for you to move. That's what Mother Teresa did.

chapter 9
the most audacious touch

*Daughter, your faith has made you well; go
in peace, and be healed of your disease.*
—Mark 5:34, NRSV

It takes a lot of nerve to have crazy faith. It's one thing to go to church. Going to church is a habit for some, a source of fellowship for others, and for still others a place to find a mate. Church often allows people to feel important and to have a voice.

For some people, church is a place to get close to God, to snuggle next to a force that brings comfort and answers to problems. Church allows people to escape from the pace and predicaments of everyday life. Church is a place where people can dress up or down and feel good about it. It's a place where children can perform in Christmas and Easter skits and make parents proud. It's a place where accomplished musicians can show off their skills. It's also a place where egos can thrive as quickly as feelings can be hurt.

Above all, it's a place where people can feel safe. Church becomes a "home" for many of us, and people take ownership. That ownership can be either toxic or healthy, but ownership it is. People are proud to be *members* of churches.

It doesn't take nerve to be a member of a church. Anybody can do that. But it does take nerve to act on your crazy faith and risk having folks believe you are just plain crazy.

If the truth be told, we are generally reluctant about proclaiming the greatness of God. We feel that we sound like fools or religious fanatics if we talk too much about God's goodness. We too often put God in a box and limit what God can do. We forget that God is creator of all things. I'm comforted when I look at the evidence of creation and understand why the psalmist wrote, "O LORD, our Lord, how excellent is thy name in all the earth!" (Psalm 8:1, KJV). One is reminded of the question that God asked Sarah when she was told that she'd have a baby at age ninety: "Is anything too hard for the LORD?" (Genesis 18:14).

Apparently, that's what we believe—that some things *are* too hard for God. So, when somebody comes along with a bold faith, we're uncomfortable. It's not fashionable to have that kind of faith. It's not sophisticated. It reveals a fair amount of ignorance. After all, everybody knows the limitations of God.

That's why crazy faith is *audacious*.

Crazy faith, spoken aloud, will make people snicker and even laugh. Crazy faith prompts people to sit back and watch, waiting to see failure. With crazy faith there are no safety nets; it's like freefalling from the sky with no parachute. It's not logical.

Think of Peter in a boat on the restless Sea of Galilee. The waves were rough, the wind was equally so, and the disciples with Peter were alone and afraid. Their fear was not assuaged when they looked and saw what appeared to be a person *walking on the water.* They were terrified and thought it was a ghost (Matthew 14:26). Jesus called out to them and told them that it was he, and they should not be afraid. But Peter was filled with fear and doubt and said, "Lord, if it's you, tell me to come to you on the water." And Jesus said, "Come" (Matthew 14:28-29).

There it is—the perfect and simple invitation to believe and to fall into the exclusive domain of those who have crazy faith. With one word, Jesus invites us: "Come."

The disciples were watching this exchange with curiosity. Yet, Peter got out of the boat. The audacity! And he began to walk toward Jesus and believed that he could. It was only when he looked down and saw what he was doing that problems arose. Fear trumped faith, and Peter began to sink.

Some of the disciples taunted him. But Jesus wasn't laughing. Jesus liked it that Peter had the audacity to walk on water. And so, as Peter began to sink and cried out to be saved, Jesus "immediately" reached out his hand and caught him (Matthew 14:31). Peter had taken his eyes off Jesus and had begun to consider why what he was doing was impossible, but Jesus had never taken his eyes off Peter.

Jesus caught Peter, but he chided him for having "little faith" (Matthew 14:31). God, through Jesus, honored Peter for being so audacious, for believing that God was greater than thought, perception, vision, and limitations. And Peter found that out by being willing to go it alone and having crazy faith. In the darkest of nights, in the midst of a storm, Peter showed by his actions that he believed.

That takes real audacity.

◎ ◎ ◎

And that's exactly what the woman in this next biblical story had: audacious faith.

There are many stories in the Bible about a particular character, especially a woman protagonist, where the person's name is never mentioned. Maybe it's intentional—an attempt to imply that the person being described could be anybody.

Whatever the reason, the woman with the issue of blood is unnamed. In all three Gospels in which the story is told (Matthew 9; Mark 5; Luke 8), she has no name and no description. She is almost an "it" with an infirmity that will not go away. Mark's rendering gives the most detail. Jesus was busy ministering, drawing great crowds wherever he went. People heard that he performed miracles, including healing, and so a great number of people clamored to see him or just be near him.

In the story, Jesus was surrounded at the time this woman appears. He actually had retired to the other side of a lake, wanting to be alone, but people saw him there and went to him. Among the people was a synagogue leader, Jairus, who fell at Jesus' feet and asked him to come home with him because his daughter was dying. "Please come," Jairus said. "Put your hands on her so that she will be healed and live" (Mark 5:23).

Jesus went with Jairus, but they weren't alone; the people continued to follow Jesus. As he walked with Jairus, the crowd grew. One might imagine that Jairus was a bit antsy; his daughter was dying, and even though Jesus knew that, he didn't seem to be in a great hurry. Jesus would stop from time to time to touch someone's forehead or grasp someone's hand. All of the people, it seemed, had their hands outstretched toward him. Jairus just hoped that Jesus' compassion for so many others didn't make them too late to reach his own daughter.

In the crowd was the unnamed woman.

We know little about her. Her story in the Bible is limited to just a few verses. But we can be sure that her story didn't begin in that crowd. Her dilemma must have begun long a time before, when she had reached puberty.[1]

She probably had begun menstruation at about the age of twelve. And, as was the custom for Hebrew women, it was a time for celebration. She, like her other young girlfriends, was called *betulah*, which meant that she had reached puberty but had not yet borne children. She would be taken by the older Hebrew women into a special tent where she was taught about life and invited to participate in the all customs practiced by pubescent girls.

Each month, when her period ended, she would have been required to wash from head to toe in a special pool called a *mikveh*. In the *mikveh* was clean water, and the pool was large enough for women to get in and be completely immersed. The women washed to get clean both physically and spiritually.

But at some point, her womanly transition took a downward turn. Her menstrual bleeding wouldn't stop. As time went on, and she was forced to remain in the woman's tent week after week, her alarm would have been shared by the other women. Perhaps her mother began to take her to doctors (see Mark 5:26). But when the doctors couldn't fix the problem, perhaps the aunts stepped in, thinking that they could do what others had not. But their efforts were futile as well. The unnamed woman found herself feeling anguished and hopeless. Where was her beloved God? Why hadn't God cured her?

She saw her peers getting married and having children, but she knew she couldn't marry. She was not an acceptable bride. The bleeding made her unclean both physically and spiritually.

◉ ◉ ◉

This was the woman who was in the crowd that blistering day when Jesus was accompanying Jairus to visit his dying daughter. The woman, in her mid-twenties by now, had been bleeding for twelve years.

The unnamed woman had heard the buzz about Jesus and his miraculous works. What manner of man was it who can do these things? He cured cripples and gave sight to the blind and hearing to the deaf. No fancy medical procedures. Just by touch. The phenomenon amazed the people and scared them, and frankly, the unnamed woman could understand why. Every doctor, every healer, had "stuff" that they pulled out to cure people. She had tried them all, but nothing had worked. The thought of a simple touch doing something was an amazing thought.

She was in her village when she heard people moving about quickly and determinedly. She looked out her window and saw people streaming from their huts, all of them moving in one direction. She called out, "Where are you going?" And someone shouted that they were going to a place near the Sea of Galilee. "The man Jesus is going to be there!"

Maybe Jesus can help me, she found herself thinking. *After all, he heals people by touching them. Maybe he can touch me.* But men didn't touch menstruating women. It was forbidden.

But perhaps she was jolted by the memory of what her mother once said: "If you believe God can, God will." And so, she joined the crowd looking for Jesus.

It was so hot, and she was so tired! The thought of this having been a futile trip crossed her mind, but by this time she had come too far to turn back. She stopped for a moment as she looked at the crowd. It was huge. How would they get to Jesus, and could he really heal all these people? But something pulsated inside of her, demanding that she not give up, not when she had come so far. She remembered the words of a psalm that her father had often quoted: "Taste and see that the LORD is good" (Psalm 34:8).

So she continued to move toward the crowd. She began to push, at first gently and then with more force. She could hear this voice, and it was tender yet strong, carrying so much power. *That has to be Jesus*, she thought. She kept pushing, by this time on her knees, crawling. Finally, she made her way to a clearing and could see Jesus. How would she get his attention? She had heard that he healed through touch, but he would not touch her, so why had she come?

The clearing had closed in, but, having seen Jesus, the young woman knew the direction in which she had to go. Still crawling on her knees, she was weak, but she was close. *If I can just touch the hem of his garment, maybe I can be healed*, she thought.

Soon she was close enough to see the wind blowing Jesus' garments. She huddled low to the ground. She began to reach for the hem. People pushed her and tried to move her away. She knew that what she was doing was crazy, and that it was a long shot to believe that touching someone's clothes would bring about healing. She inched closer, stretching as far as she could, until finally she was able to reach the hem. When she touched Jesus' garment, immediately the bleeding in her body stopped, and her suffering was over (Mark 5:28-29).

There was no more bleeding. It was so complete a cessation of pain that it startled her. She wanted to get up and shout, but she couldn't, not because she was unable, but because she was too stunned. She was healed.

Just as she was about to turn and crawl back out of the crowd, she heard Jesus say, "Who touched my clothes?" (Mark 5:30).

When she touched him, Jesus had felt power leave his body. This touch had been intentional, and there was a spirit-to-spirit connection. The unnamed woman stood, trembling, and looked at Jesus. She felt hot, angry, resentful stares on her from the disciples, from strangers, from people who knew her. "The audacity of that woman!" she heard the wife of one of the rabbis snap. "Who does she think she is?"

She lowered her eyes and approached Jesus. "It was me," she said timidly. She fell at his feet, telling him how she had suffered for twelve years, how the doctors had been unable to cure her, and how she had no friends. When she paused, Jesus walked toward her and touched her. She recoiled because nobody had really touched her for twelve years.

Lifting her face by cupping her chin in his hands, he said gently, "Daughter, your faith has healed you. Go in peace and be freed from your suffering" (Mark 5:34).

She couldn't figure which moved her more: the physical healing or the spiritual transformation and empowerment. But she knew for certain that she was different from that moment on. She had tasted and seen that the Lord was good, and she was humbled as much as she was overjoyed and overcome.

Crazy faith made her believe a simple touch could heal. It was an audacious move, and it had made her whole.

☉ ☉ ☉

Meanwhile, Jairus was still waiting for Jesus to heal his daughter. He was sure by now that she had died. If the truth be told, he was angry at this strange woman for interrupting Jesus and taking his time. As they got near his house, Jairus's stomach turned when he heard the sound of wailing. The professional wailers had begun their work because his daughter had died. Jairus knew that Jesus could heal the sick, but raise the dead? That was unheard of. As they neared the door, some of the men approached him and said, "Your daughter is dead. Why bother the teacher any more?" (Mark 5:35).

Jairus's face fell, and he began to sob. Jesus turned to him and said, "Don't be afraid; just believe" (Mark 5:36). *Believe what?* Jairus must have wondered as they made their way inside the house. His little girl was dead. What was he supposed to believe?

His mind went back to the woman who had just been healed. She had believed that touching Jesus would heal her, and it did. Was he really to have faith like that? Believe that a touch could bring about life from death?

When Jesus entered, he sounded irritated and annoyed as he shut the professional wailers down. "Why all this commotion and wailing?" he asked crossly. "The child is not dead but asleep" (Mark 5:39). They laughed at him, but Jesus ignored them and sent them all out of the house, except for the girl's parents and his disciples.

He took Jairus and his wife and the disciples who had accompanied him to the house, and they approached the little girl. The mother was sobbing uncontrollably. And Jairus was truly angry at Jesus for having taken so long to get to his house and to his problem. Now he was wrestling with what Jesus had commanded him: "Don't be afraid; just believe."

Then Jesus took the girl's hand and said, *"Talitha koum!"* which means, "Little girl, I say to you, get up!" (Mark 5:41). And immediately, the girl stood up and walked around (Mark 5:42).

Life had come from death because of crazy, crazy faith, this time on the part of Jesus, who, like the unnamed woman, believed that God is a true healer. The unnamed woman really represents all of us. Her character is universal. The story that you have just read is my account based on the biblical story and my imagination. The unnamed woman's power is evident by the faith that she had and by her desire to be healed and made whole.

Crazy, audacious faith!

Crazy-Faith Challenge

Doctors have incredible knowledge and skills, but their abilities are finite. In the midst of the most horrible of prognoses, we have a choice to buy into what the doctor says or to save a bit of our emotions to invest in the belief that God can do what people cannot. It is a fact that our spirits affect those closest to us, as well as ourselves. The importance of a faith-fed spirit cannot be overrated. It is as though the darkness of a serious illness and the gloom that it brings are being blown away by light that comes from faith. Even if a complete physical healing doesn't happen, a spiritual healing in the midst of despair is still a miracle.

The doctor says it's over, and your time is done. What does your faith say?

chapter 10
the eighth wonder of the world

*It was one of those occasions when the hand
of man had enhanced that
already wrought by the hand of God.*
—David McCullough

John Roebling would not have impressed anyone as being a particularly religious man by today's standards, but he believed in God and was interested in what he called "spiritualism." He was brilliant, and he credited God with giving him that gift. He felt that his job was to give back to God by using that intellect.

Born in 1806 in Germany, Roebling was a musician, scholar, architect, engineer, philosopher, and perpetual student. He had a hunger to learn, and he worked to develop his mind in every way he could. His love for learning helped him succeed at the famed Royal Polytechnic Institute in Berlin, where he studied engineering. He left that school with a love for building bridges. What he studied about their construction fascinated him, but he didn't think that he would get the experience and opportunities that he needed if he stayed in Europe—there were enough bridges there already. America to him was virgin territory; so armed with his passion for bridges and a conviction that he would build great ones, he headed for America.

Nobody could see bridges like he could. He dreamed of building grand bridges, not like anything that had been done before. If one had a vision in mind, he believed, and the capability to do it, then one did it. Because of his belief in spiritualism, there was always the suggestion that a power from somewhere would provide help. One must always find the way to make the vision happen, he believed. He said, "If one plan won't do, then another must."[1]

His biggest dream, or vision, was to build a bridge over the East River from New York City to Brooklyn. When he arrived in the United States, there was no way for people to get from New York City to Brooklyn except by ferry. The vision must have been in his spirit, but it was actually birthed when he took the ferry with his fifteen-year-old son, Washington, one winter day in 1852 and grew irritated. The day was so cold that the river was filled with ice, and it took the ferry forever to get to the other side. It was on that day that he told his son that there must be a bridge built between the two cities.[2]

The idea was preposterous. By this time, Roebling had built other bridges and was known to do good work. The longest bridge that he had built up to that point was a suspension bridge between Cincinnati, Ohio, and Covington, Kentucky. So he was known to be an able engineer.

But the thought of a bridge over the East River was another thing. The East River was known for its swift, violent, and unpredictable currents. It would be the largest suspension bridge in the world. It would have to cross the East River in one piece and be high enough for great ships on their way into the Atlantic to safely pass. And the bridge would have to be sturdy enough to withstand the strong winds that plagued the river.

Roebling could see it in his mind: it would cross the river "with one uninterrupted central span, held aloft by huge cables slung from the tops of two colossal stone towers and secured on either shore to massive masonry piles called anchorages."[3] The anchorages would be seven stories tall—taller than most buildings at the time—and would take up a good part of a New York City block. There would be two twin towers, each 268 feet high, their distinctive marks being two Gothic arches, two in each tower.[4] Below the water, the towers would be made of limestone and built on two huge wooden structures called "caissons," which would be gradually sunk into the East River until they reached bedrock. These caissons would be strong enough to hold the towers, each of which would weigh 67,850 tons standing alone, but with the added weight of a planned roadway on the bridge, each caisson would bear 72,603 tons.[5] And its length: from one end to the other, the "Great Bridge," as people were calling it, would measure 5,862 feet—more than a mile.[6]

It was a preposterous proposition. People couldn't believe what they were hearing. Sure, a bridge was necessary, but how would such a thing be built? It would never work. It would crash and cause undue injury, misery, and death. But Roebling had an unshakable, crazy vision that it would work, and he would not back away from the vision. In fact, in addition to the bridge having a roadway that pedestrians as well as horses and carriages could cross, Roebling proposed to build railroad tracks to accommodate trains.

By 1869, approval for construction of the bridge became a reality. All the while he built bridges, and all the while he was drawing up the plans for the Great Bridge, Roebling taught his craft to his young son, Washington, who was also an aspiring engineer. The two of them built their first bridge together in 1858. Washington actually supervised most of the job. Washington worked alongside his father in the building of the Cincinnati Bridge, a project that took ten years to complete. The two of them also worked on the suspension bridge at Niagara Falls, a bridge that "seemed to make the whole breath-taking panorama all the more terrifying, all the more magnificent. It was one of those occasions when the hand of man had enhanced that already wrought by the hand of God," says author David McCullough.[7]

All this time spent with his father watching him, working with him, instructing, and guiding him proved to be propitious for young Washington. In June of 1869, some seventeen years after John Roebling had begun his journey to get the Great Bridge out of his mind and onto the East River, the plans were approved and work was to begin. But on June 28, 1869, Roebling, out on the site where the first caisson would be built, was struck by a boat as he stood on a pile. The accident resulted in his foot being crushed.

After the injury, Roebling's toes had to be amputated. For a while, it seemed to be on the mend. But then tetanus set in. He suffered, and his son watched as the muscles in John's face, neck, and jaw became rigid with pain. He was unable to eat, and then he began having seizures.

In spite of his physical pain, his mind remained clear, and he never stopped talking about the bridge. His son and everyone who saw him were amazed. This was a vision given to him by God, and the way to honor God was to use his intellect and build.

On July 21, he was well enough to be lifted from his bed. He began to sketch, telling his assistants and his son how the bridge was to be done. He worked feverishly, the vision pushing through his very veins. He issued orders throughout the night, scribbling notes and making sketches.

But at 3:00 a.m., he suffered a convulsion "so violent that he leaped clear from the bed" and had to be caught by one of his assistants in the room.[8]

Minutes later, he was dead, and now the work of building the Great Bridge lay before Washington Roebling, the son and student who had learned from his father so many important things about engineering and bridge building, but also so many things about making the impossible happen. Now Washington would have to show the world how crazy faith really worked.

◉ ◉ ◉

Washington's wife, Emily, has been described as beautiful and intelligent and as possessing "a scientific bent of mind."[9] Little did Washington know then how much her intellect would help him as construction of the bridge progressed. Washington, who eventually became confined to bed from illness, began dictating directions and instructions to Emily, which she in turn took to the construction crew and engineers. That those men listened to and respected her is nothing short of miraculous. Her husband watched the construction of the bridge from his bedroom window, and he would feverishly write down all the things that needed to happen and give those notes to Emily. She would take the notes from her husband to the staff and explain to them what was to be done. Emily would bring reports back to her husband from the engineers. Not a bit of work was done on the Brooklyn Bridge without Washington Roebling's specific instructions, brought to the crew by Emily.

Washington's illness came about from his involvement in the bridge's construction. The most innovative feature of the Brooklyn Bridge was its being built on huge wooden caissons. These caissons would support the bridge towers, each of which reached 276½ feet above the water. The caissons would have to be sunk to the bottom of the river, sitting on bedrock. These caissons were by far the largest ever built and would have to go deeper than any others to date. On the Brooklyn side, the caisson was sunk 44½ feet, but on the New York City side, the caisson had to be sunk a remarkable 78½ feet.

The men working in the caissons endured horrible conditions. Their work space was hot and small, and the temperature was estimated at times to be in the mid-90s. The air that they breathed had to be pressurized because of the great depths to which they were descending. When the men came up from the caisson, many of them became sick, getting the bends—what they called "caisson disease." They didn't know that after having been so deep underground, using pressurized air to survive, they needed ample time for their bodies to readjust as they came up to the normal air pressure. The result of coming up from the caissons too quickly was that they became sick, developing severe and mysterious pain, and sometimes paralysis.

Having stayed in the caissons for long periods of time, Washington himself had suffered bouts of the bends. But he had always fought his way through it and gone back to his work. It was another incident that proved to be a turning point both for Washington and Emily Roebling, and for the future and completion of the bridge.

A fire erupted in the New York caisson. Washington Roebling was on the site as soon as he heard about the fire. Hoses were first put in crevices between the wood to try to extinguish the fire, but it wasn't effective. The best way to insure that the fire was out was to flood the caisson, but that had to be a last resort. And so he stayed in the caisson for hours, way too long, according to written accounts. One wonders if he thought about his father, so critically ill with tetanus and still working, as he worked in the caisson, tired and sick.

About 5:00 a.m., after he decided that the fire was out, he left. Moments after he breathed in the fresh air, Roebling began to experience paralysis.[10] He was carried home, and "for the next three hours he was rubbed vigorously all over with a solution of salt and whiskey."[11] After a while, he regained the use of his legs. The experience had left him weak, but able to walk.

Three hours later, one of the workers came to his house and told him that the fire was still burning, and Washington got dressed and went back to the caisson. He spent more hours in the caisson, finally resorting to flooding it to put the fire completely out. He had managed to save his beloved bridge, but his body had taken a beating, and it would not recover.

He continued to work on the bridge, spending twelve to fourteen hours a day, six days a week, in the caissons. On Sundays he went to church. He was weak and in pain much of the time, but nothing could keep him away from the site. The New York City caisson was proving to be the greatest challenge, a challenge from which Roebling would not back away. On May 18, 1872, with the caisson now sunk to a depth of 78½ feet, Roebling decided that they had gone deep enough. They had not reached bedrock, but the sand on which it sat was solid. More and more of his workers were getting sick, and Roebling's decision might have been predicated on the fact that on the day before he ordered the digging to stop, one of his men had gotten critically ill coming out of the caisson and died.

It was enough. If God wanted this bridge to be built, it was going to be at this depth. It was simply enough.

While the caisson was being filled with concrete, Roebling suffered another attack of the bends, collapsing and lying close to death in the same house in which his father had died.[12] Although John Roebling had not been a very religious man, he had understood the importance of holding on to something higher than one's own emotions and fears—what I'm calling "crazy faith." "The great secret," John Roebling had said, is to "keep off fear."

Despite Washington Roebling's dogged faith that he would get better, his doctors said otherwise. And Emily knew it. They told her that she should be "prepared for the worst," and that although he was obsessed with seeing the bridge finished, that probably would not happen. She watched him as he spent that winter "writing down all that had to be done, filling page after page with the most exacting, painstaking directions for making the cables, for assembling the complicated components of the superstructure, and illustrating these with detailed freehand drawings and diagrams."[13]

It was a good thing, because by now he was no longer able to go to the bridge site. The two towers stood on either side of the river, begging for completion of the glorious legacy that they were destined to become. But Washington was confined to his room, eyes failing, and he was having difficulty writing and periodically was experiencing paralysis. He and Emily traveled to Europe to see other doctors and receive more and different treatment. Their hope was that something would produce a change in Washington so that he could be on the site of the bridge.

But that was not to be. The baton, which had first been passed from John to his son Washington, was now passed by Washington to his wife, Emily. The completion of the Brooklyn Bridge was in her hands.

Emily began to immerse herself in bridge building, learning all that she could so that as her husband dictated, she would have her own understanding of what he was saying. She was facing her own Goliath. Her husband was an invalid, and the truth of the matter was that "hers was the real mind behind the great work" and that "the most monumental engineering triumph of the age was actually the doing of a woman."[14] Emily knew that gossip, naysaying, and criticism were flying around, but she also knew her husband. She knew his faith and determination not to give up. Emily Roebling "had a quick and retentive mind, a natural gift for mathematics, and she had been a diligent student," not only during the time she had been married, but also as her husband became sicker. Illness was not going to stop this bridge. Both she and her husband were resolute on that fact.

And so the years of building the bridge from the window in Brooklyn began, Washington dictating to Emily, she writing his instructions and then taking the technical information to the engineers on the site. When bridge officials and engineers went to the

Roebling house to ask questions or get instructions or direction, it was seldom Washington who greeted them—rather it was Emily.[15] "She would carry on an interview in his behalf, asking questions and answering theirs with perfect confidence and command of the facts."[16] They left her satisfied that they had met with whom they needed, and they expressed complete confidence in Emily and her knowledge and skills.

Emily stayed with and ensured success of the building of the bridge for eleven years, acting as surrogate chief engineer. Without her, the bridge would not have been completed. Who would have thought that such a bridge could be built, through the intermediary supervision of a woman, as her husband, the chief engineer, sat from his window and watched? Who would have thought that men of that time would even listen to her, and that she would be able to navigate the sexism that followed her daily? She was skilled beyond anything anyone could have imagined. Once, when a manufacturer had been puzzled by how a particular part of the superstructure should be done, it was Emily, having studied her husband's drawings, who explained the process to the manufacturer and each step that he should take.[17] When the last part of the superstructure was in place in May of 1883, it was Emily who rode a carriage across to prove the strength of the bridge to those who watched nervously. "She and a coachman crossed over from Brooklyn in a new victoria, its varnish gleaming in the sunshine. She had taken a live rooster with her, as a symbol of victory."[18]

When the bridge officially opened on May 20, 1883, both Emily and Washington must have stopped and thanked God for the miracle that had been birthed before their eyes. For believing in the impossible, God had allowed the most amazing victory: the completion of a suspension bridge, the largest at the time in the world over one of the most trying rivers in this nation, a symbol of glory as well as progress.

And God had allowed it to be completed by an invalid man who watched from his window as his wife, a woman named Emily, completed the Eighth Wonder of the World.

Crazy-Faith Challenge

There always comes a time in life when something insurmountable happens and we get "thrown for a loop." When the loops in your life hit, what do you do? Do you look for God and expect God to help you past the obstacle, or do you fall into despair? Do you become a spiritual invalid? The Roeblings—father, son, and daughter-in-law—continued to be thrown for loops. But they rallied; neither sickness nor sexism nor death stopped them, because they had dreams—dreams that had to be fulfilled. They had a bridge to build. What dreams has God placed on your heart? What is your bridge, and how will you build it?

chapter 11
how shall they eat?

But he answered them,
"You give them something to eat."
—Mark 6:37, NRSV

To the disciples, it must have looked like a multicolored quilt covering the mountainside.

The disciples, along with Jesus, had crossed to the far side of the Sea of Galilee. Jesus told them to rest, and they wholeheartedly agreed. And then Jesus, as was his custom, retreated from them to pray.

They welcomed the opportunity to get away from the people, to chat together and share all the things that they were seeing and learning. Being with Jesus was proving to be life-changing, and they found that they needed time to digest all that they experienced.

Imagine their surprise when, as they were talking and resting, the disciples heard the voices of people coming from the direction of the port at the sea. Peter sent one of the disciples to see what was going on, and to their amazement, the people were coming across the sea to be near Jesus. They had gotten on boats and rafts, and they were coming in droves. Not only that, but as the reporting disciple looked around on his way back to the place where Jesus and the others were, he could see people coming over the mountainside from every direction. Some were walking, some were crawling. Some were carrying others.

The disciples were growing worried. Jesus had preached before big crowds, but this one seemed to be growing larger than any they had ever seen. They hiked to a point on the mountain to which they had retreated and were awed.

There were so many people that the grass couldn't be seen beneath them. "How many people *are* there?" Peter asked aloud.

"Thousands," replied another. "Thousands. And they just keep coming."

The disciples began to mobilize and delineate tasks. And Jesus, for his part, was moved, not because of the numbers of people, but because of the need that the people represented. There were more poor people than rich, more people who had needs that had never been met. Jesus had compassion and began healing the sick (Matthew 14:14).

Of course, Jesus' acts of healing only increased the crowd. He had healed hundreds of people as the disciples watched the tear-stained, grateful faces of those who had been touched and healed.

After a while, Jesus began to preach and to teach. The hot sun was setting, and still the people were coming. Peter estimated that there were at least *five thousand men*, plus women and children. As Jesus stopped talking to take a sip of water, the disciples seized an opportunity. "Jesus," they said, "it's getting late, and this is a remote place. Send these people away so they can buy something to eat."

Jesus looked at Philip, one of the disciples, and asked him, "Where shall we buy bread for these people to eat?" (John 6:5). The question was only a test; he was asking Philip, but this was a teaching moment for all the disciples.

Philip's sentiments were echoed by all of the other disciples: "Eight months' wages would not buy enough bread for each one to have a bite!" (John 6:7).

Jesus smiled. The angst of the disciples would have to be addressed. They, those who were closest to him, would have to be reminded of who he was, what he was doing, and from whom he got his authority. They were just like the wilderness crowd that Moses had led. They would have to be reminded that with God, nothing is impossible.

"Please remember this," Jesus said gently. "Whoever believes has eternal life. I am the bread of life. Your forefathers ate the manna in the desert, yet they died" (John 6:47-49). Jesus reminded them of how there were masses of Israelites in the wilderness who had grown afraid and angry and actually said that they would rather have died in Egypt than be in the wilderness. Jesus reminded his disciples that God was with them, and they would not be hungry. They forgot about the manna that God had rained down for them and later the quail; and they didn't remember how when God gave them the food that they desired, they complained, and still God was with them (Exodus 16; Numbers 11). They forgot about all the times God had rescued and saved them. "You cannot forget; you must remember and teach and remind the people," Jesus must have said, looking out over the massive crowd. "I know that it's late and that there are a lot of people out there, but God is here. They will eat because God is here."

Jesus welcomed a small boy who had five loaves of bread and two fish. He asked the child to bring the food to him. "The people will eat," Jesus said calmly.

All right, the disciples thought, *you have in front of you five barley loaves, and they're small, and two little fish.* The disciples knew that any one of them could devour that small amount of food in minutes. Were there more fish, or was there perhaps a bread vendor around? Some of them began to look, but Jesus stopped them. "There is no more—just this," he said. And seeing the doubt on their faces, he said, "We don't have a lot of food, but we have God."

It was so hard to get with Jesus on this one. He had healed people, and that was good, but this was different. There was no way those five loaves and two fish were going to feed what looked to be—counting men, women, and children—about ten thousand people. The disciples admired Jesus' faith, but this was a stretch. Yes, God was good, but the facts were the facts. Five barley loaves and two fish were not going to cut it. *Somebody should tell Jesus,* thought one of the disciples, *before he does something really stupid and gets this crowd riled up.*

Jesus knew what they were thinking, but he ignored them. He asked them to sit down. They needed to *see* how God would show up when and if his children believed that he could. Jesus knew that the proportion of food to the number of people before him was skewed, but he also knew that God—the same God who had been with Moses and parted the Red Sea—was here. God would feed the people.

Jesus stood before them, holding one of the five barley loaves and the two fish. Slowly, he lifted the bread and fish toward heaven and began to thank God.

As he did so, there was a rumbling in the crowd. The disciples looked on, amazed, as people began to rummage through their belongings. Food began to appear. They had brought some with them, most of them. As each person got food in his or her hands, they, like Jesus, lifted their food toward heaven and began to thank God. *They took out their food and imitated Jesus.* The disciples squirmed. All over the side of that mountain, hands were raised toward heaven. They did exactly as Jesus did. When he had given thanks, he broke the bread and offered it to his disciples. And the people, when they had given thanks, broke their bread and looked around to see who had none and shared.

The people shared. It was the first communion of saints. It was also a miracle.[1]

Jesus was not teaching the people to do anything different than what he himself was required to do. He had said it over and over: his work and power came from God. There were things that God had asked him to do that had been absolutely stupid when thought of in terms of human ability to conceptualize—for instance, when he turned water into wine, and when he raised Lazarus from the dead. People didn't realize, not even his disciples, that the more he had faith in God, the more faith he was fed by God. On one occasion they had told him to eat, and he said in response, "My food is to do the will of him who sent me and to finish his work" (John 4:34).

The disciples didn't understand, but Jesus had been concerned about what God was telling him. How was it possible, he had thought, for these loaves and fish to feed this many people? But he had heard his heavenly Father telling him to trust. As Jesus had lifted the bread and fish toward heaven, God had said to him, "The people will be fed. If you believe, the people will be fed." It could have been an unbearable moment for Jesus, until he allowed his mind to go back to Moses and his wilderness experience and allowed himself to remember that with God, nothing is impossible. At that moment, he relaxed and said that God's purposes would be done. He did not know *how* the people would be fed, but only *that* they would be fed.

When Jesus had given thanks and then looked away from heaven toward the crowd, his eyes filled with tears. People where sharing, talking, and helping each other. Food seemed to be coming from everywhere. He looked at his disciples, and they were eating. Jesus' crazy faith had been rewarded. What he had believed had become real.

After all had had their fill, there was food left over. Jesus could hear his disciples' amazement as they looked around and saw that so much was left. Jesus told them, "Gather the pieces that are left over. Let nothing be wasted" (John 6:12). The disciples borrowed baskets from women who had brought with them belongings, including food, and began to gather the remains.

Twelve baskets were filled. Another miracle.

☉ ☉ ☉

To God, it must look like a multicolored quilt.

Poor people cover the globe in massive numbers. In spite of great resources, every country has an abundance of poor people, and the attitude of those who are not so poor is that the problem is too big for anyone to fix.

On a recent trip to Ghana, West Africa, my then sixteen-year-old son sat silently on the musty bus that was transporting us. Although the people were friendly and the children's eyes were full of hope and enthusiasm, the poverty was rampant and discouraging. We saw people sleeping on concrete porches with no cot or cover. Others we saw lying on the dusty ground. There were few roads, no potable water, none of the conveniences to which we have grown accustomed in the United States. At one point, I heard my son whisper, "The poverty! The people are so poor!"

It distressed him, but the fact is that poverty covers the globe. What we saw in West Africa might be considered mild compared to the poverty in other places in the world. Muhammad Yunus, who won the Nobel Peace Prize in 2006, said in his acceptance speech, "Ninety-four percent of the world's income goes to 40 percent of the population while 60 percent of people live on only 6 percent of world income." He further noted that one-half of the world's population lives on two dollars a day, and over one billion people live on less than one dollar a day.[2]

When one looks at the conditions that people live in, it's easy to become discouraged and to believe, as the disciples did on the day that more than five thousand were fed, that nothing can be done. In fact, many believe that some people are just meant to be poor.

More than that, though, humans are apt to become overwhelmed by the conditions of poverty, forgetting that if God exists, poverty does not have to. Yunus won the Nobel Peace Prize because he could no longer stand looking at the vast numbers of poor people while teaching the principles of economics. His heart was pricked, and the fact that these people were ostracized, marginalized, ignored, and despised bothered him. In his acceptance speech, Yunus stated that "poverty is not created by poor people."[3] It is the way the economic system is set up, making it virtually impossible for the poor to get out of their situations. Yunus said that he couldn't ignore the "crushing hunger and poverty" that he saw all around him.[4]

The people need "feeding." Millions of people, all over the world, are hungry for dignity and a chance for a new life. Yunus tried to get banks to loan money to poor people, which the banks would not do because they see poor people as a bad credit risk. And the fact that the poor and the suffering still existed in the midst of a *religious* world disturbed Yunus.

With God, nothing is impossible.

There is no evidence to suggest that Yunus is Christian, but he does believe in God, and one might suppose that it was God speaking to his heart that ultimately provided him with a way to minister to the people whose plight bothered him. Maybe he lifted the situation up to God and gave thanks and asked for help.

The answer came in the form of the Grameen Bank, formed in Bangladesh and now spread all over the world. The bank decided to give small loans to poor people, mostly women because they have the responsibility of raising the children, to help them get on their feet, form a business that will help them get out of poverty and stay out of poverty, and then pay the money back.

The results have been no less miraculous than the feeding of the more than five thousand. To date, the bank has given loans to over seven million poor people, 97 percent of whom are women.

The bank gives out thirty thousand scholarships annually to the children of these women so that they can go to school. The bank's housing loans have been used to construct over six hundred thousand houses.[5] The actions of *one man* have helped literally millions of people.

One might surmise that as Yunus began his project, people around him doubted both the possibility of making a difference and the wisdom of engaging in such a task. Yet, he pressed on. There was a wilderness crowd before him, but he was called to be a Moses and lead the people out.

Those who have benefited from Muhammad Yunus's project have shared their wisdom. And person-by-person, rampant poverty is being addressed and dealt with. Like Jesus feeding the multitude, it's a project that could come only from crazy faith.

Crazy-Faith Challenge

When we can articulate a huge problem, one so big that everyone can see it but few people feel competent to address it, we often bury our faith in the grave of practicality. We believe that some problems are just too big for us to handle. How many social problems in our communities have we ignored because we were afraid of the great work that God planted in us? In fact, how many of us actually doubt that God could or would use us in such a way? Mother Teresa and Muhammad Yunus allowed God to work with them and through them. Could you be so bold, and would you let God use you?

chapter 12
the scales fell from my eyes

*Though I hadn't a penny, I had faith in a living
God, faith in myself and a desire to serve.*
—Mary McLeod Bethune

When I was little, I remember hearing a song called "High
Hopes." Written by Jimmy Van Heusen and Sammy Cahn in
1959 for the movie *A Hole in the Head*, the song was made pop-
ular through the smooth voice of Frank Sinatra, and it won the
Academy Award that year for Best Original Song.

> Just what makes that little old ant
> Think he can move that rubber tree plant
> Anyone knows an ant can't
> Move a rubber tree plant
>
> But he's got high hopes, he's got high hopes
> He's got high, apple pie, in the sky hopes[1]

It was a silly song, but the words stuck with me. As Sinatra
sang, I would sing with him, bellowing as loud as I could. I could
literally *see* an ant trying to move a rubber tree plant. I didn't
even know what a rubber tree plant was, but I knew it had to be
pretty big to be worthy of mention that an ant had moved it.

I realize now that the song was talking about crazy faith. It was by no means a religious song, but it involved crazy faith nonetheless. That little song showed how powerful faith is and proved that having crazy faith really does empower the one who is doing the believing. Because of high hopes—crazy faith—and the ram and the ant, the impossible becomes possible and real.

Making the impossible become possible and then real was the forte of Mary McLeod Bethune.

⊚ ⊚ ⊚

She was a little slave girl, the fifteenth of seventeen children born to Samuel and Patsy McLeod. By the time she was nine years old, she could pick 250 pounds of cotton a day.

Mary Jane McLeod was born in 1875 in Mayesville, South Carolina, twelve years after the Emancipation Proclamation. No doubt, things were "better" for people of African descent because slavery was outlawed by then. And African Americans— "Negroes" then—were working to determine and chart the courses of their destiny. Life was hard, but the newly freed slaves were optimistic about the possibilities that existed for them in a country still hostile toward them.

Mary's family kept in close contact with the people who had owned them as slaves. Her mother, whose "will power and drive" gave the McLeod family the inspiration and encouragement, continued to work for her former master until she had earned five acres of land.[2]

Mary's spirit came straight from her mother, a woman of unshakable faith and whose optimism kept the family afloat. She garnered her fierce sense of pride from her mother, who had come from African royalty. Mary says of her mother, "She could not be discouraged. No matter what kind of plight we found ourselves in, she always believed there was, through prayer and work, a way out."³ That must have seemed miraculous to Mary. How could a woman with seventeen children and not enough money never be discouraged? How was she able to work as hard as she did, suffer the continued indignities of black people, and never give up? She simply worked and prayed and taught her children to do the same.

Mary felt the disparity between herself and the little white children with whom she worked and played. It did something to her to be with these children and then have to stand aside and watch them go to school. "I could see little white boys and girls going to school every day, learning to read and write, living in comfortable homes with all types of opportunities for growth and service, and to be surrounded as I was with no opportunity for school life, no chance to grow—I found myself very often yearning all along for the things that were being provided for the white children with whom I had to chop cotton every day, or pick corn, or whatever my task happened to be."⁴

Mary yearned to learn. None of her siblings and none of her friends could read. At that time, it was not only crazy and unrealistic for black children to want to learn to read and write, but also illegal. Mary recalled that fact being made plain to her one day, and it was the spark that she needed to push her forward and upward.

Her mother, in keeping her relationship with her former owners intact, often took Mary with her to the big house. "I remember my mother went over to do some special work for this family of Wilsons, and I was with her." Mary recalled. "I went out into what they called their playhouse in the yard where they did their studying. They had pencils, slates, magazines, and books. I picked up one of the books…and one of the girls said to me, 'You can't read that! Put that down!'" Mary said that the girl's comments stung her to her soul. "It just did something to my pride and to my heart." But contrary to killing her spirit and drive, that girl's comment made Mary determined that "some day I would read just as she was reading."[5]

Mary kept her eyes and ears open for her opportunity, for there was no doubt in her mind that God, knowing her desire to learn, would make it happen. She said that one day, while the family was out in the field picking cotton, Emma Wilson "the mission teacher came from Mayesville...and told mother and father that the Presbyterian Church had established a mission where the Negro children could go and that the children would be allowed to go."[6]

Mary's heart leapt for joy. She determined that God had heard her prayer and had seen her vision. She was going to learn, and God was making it happen.

On her first day at the Mayesville school, Mary listened as Emma Wilson opened the Bible to John 3:16 and read to the class: "For God so loved the world, that he gave his only begotten Son, that whosoever believeth in him should not perish, but have everlasting life." Mary later recalled that upon hearing those words, "The scales fell from my eyes, and the light came flooding in. My sense of inferiority, my fear of handicaps, dropped away. 'Whosoever,' it said....It meant that I, a humble Negro girl, had as much chance as anybody in the sight and love of God. These words stored up a battery of faith and confidence and determination, which has not failed me."[7]

Mary loved being in school. As she learned, she felt empowered and no longer shackled by a society that did not believe in her worth. She knew that God had something for her to do. Her task was to find out what it was and do it. On Sunday afternoons she would gather all the children who worked on the farms for miles around and teach them what she was learning. "As I got, I gave," she said.[8] She taught them poetry, songs, and the stories that she had learned to read. Their excitement in learning made her even more eager to learn and to share. When she was able to read the Bible and magazines to her parents, she began teaching her older brother. Mary didn't realize it, but part of the plan for her life was to teach. Her brother was so inspired by what she was teaching him that he would walk six miles from the family farm to Mayesville so that he could attend night school. He did that until he could read, write, and "apply himself."[9]

Mary's aptitude for math made her extremely useful to her family and to the white business people with whom her family dealt. She was soon called upon to determine the weights of cotton picked and the prices to be assigned. The more she believed she could do, the more she could do, and she made it her business to use whatever she learned to help others. "I made my learning, what little it was, just from the beginning, spell service and cooperation, rather than something that would put me above the people around me," she said.[10]

In retrospect, Mary found it amazing that she was able to do so much despite not being the best or smartest in her class. She recalled making plenty of mistakes, but she kept her eyes on God and her ears inclined toward God, whom she was sure had put her where she wanted and needed to be. Her focus was on the certainty that God had a plan for her life. One day, Mary knew that she would have what others had.

Mary had been in the Mayesville school for five years when a visiting Presbyterian minister told her parents that a white woman in Denver, Colorado, heard of the wonderful work that Emma Wilson had done with the town's Negro children and wondered if there was a young girl in the school who the teachers felt would benefit from furthering her education. The woman, Mary Chrisman, who was a teacher, sponsored the Presbyterian Church Project for slave children and would be paying all expenses.

The teachers chose Mary Jane McLeod. When Mary's parents told her that she had been chosen to go Scotia Seminary in Concord, North Carolina, she could hardly believe her ears.

Mary immersed herself in her new surroundings, soaking up everything she could. It was different than the school at Mayesville, where the student population was all black. At Scotia, almost all the students were white. There were both black and white teachers, who talked together, ate together, and appeared to genuinely respect each other. Mary paid close attention to all that she saw and was certain that it was necessary for what God had planned.

She appreciated her educational opportunity and no longer felt inadequate. Mary felt that her talents were being used and appreciated. She felt that her intellect was being honored, and this made her more confident. God had revealed that the world's opinion of her was a direct contradiction of God's opinion of her and her people, and this gave her pause and joy. Being a woman of confidence was far away from being a woman who did not know her worth. It was a lesson that Mary cherished in her heart.

Mary graduated from Scotia with the equivalent of an associate's degree from a junior college, and a week later, she took a train to Chicago to attend the Moody Bible Institute. She was the only African American among the eleven hundred students. She attended Moody because she wanted desperately to be a missionary in Africa, but she was told upon completion of her work that there were no places in Africa where the school could "place a Negro." She was placed in Augusta, Georgia, instead, as a teacher at the Haines Normal and Industrial Institute. Though disappointed, she did her mission work with zeal. It was all a part of God's plan for her life. It was while Mary was at Haines that she realized how much missionary work was needed in America with poor, black children. After a year, she transferred to the Kindell Institute in Sumter, South Carolina. It was there that she met the man she eventually married, Albertus Bethune.

By now, Mary knew what God wanted her to do, and it became a burning passion. She wanted to build a school for black girls. After her son Albert was born, she stopped teaching for a year, but her vision was clear. Her husband couldn't understand. He wondered how she, a black woman in America with no money, could build a school. She tried patiently to explain how God had been with her guiding her path. "It was for this, Albertus," she would say. "I don't know how I'll build the school. I just know I will build it."

Albertus considered himself a religious man, but this thing his wife talked about sounded crazy—impractical and impossible. A tension developed between them because her crazy faith and his lack of faith took its toll on their marriage. He had gone with her to Florida, the place where she eventually decided she would build her school. Mary's drive was fueled by stories she heard from blacks who had gone to Palatka, Florida, to help build the Florida East Coast railroad. The black people worked hard, but they experienced discrimination in all areas of their lives, including education. Mary's resolve was strengthened, but Albertus decided that he'd had enough. The couple never divorced, but by 1900 they had gone their separate ways.

Undaunted, Mary moved forward with her young son. In 1904 they "hitched a ride with railway workers" from Palatka to Daytona Beach, and what she saw there made her know that Daytona was the place for her school.[11] There were scores of black people filled with hopelessness and seeing no way out of their misery. Here was a whole city of her people in need of what she'd been given. Mary knew that it was her time, her place, and her opportunity.

Still, she wondered how would she do it? There were no wealthy lenders waiting to hand her money to build a school. There were no banks willing to take a risk. She had no money and no advantages, and she knew it. But she had God.

She went looking for the location for her school and found "an old abandoned cottage on the edge of the city dump."[12] Neither the location nor the state of the cottage discouraged her. With crazy-faith fervor, "she persuaded the white owner of the cottage to rent it to her."13

On October 3, 1904, she opened the Daytona Educational and Industrial Training School for Negro Girls. She opened with her own son and five little girls whose parents paid her 50 cents a week. For pencils, she burned logs and used the charred splinters, and for ink, she used juice from mashed elderberries. She would ask strangers for things that she needed for the school, and often she was seen frequenting the city dump looking for anything that could be salvaged. Her passion and faith made her see. "Though I hadn't a penny, ...I had faith in a living God, faith in myself and a desire to serve," she said.14

The school grew exponentially. In less than two years it had more than 250 students and had been chartered as the Daytona Normal and Industrial Institute for Negro Scholars.15 Mary had some volunteers and some teachers who were paid from $15 to $25 a month, and she was always devising projects to make money for the fledgling school, including choir concerts, bake sales, dress sales—anything that would help fill the hole that represented the school's need for funds. She was neither afraid nor discouraged. She never missed an opportunity to push for the needs of her school, because she considered it God's school, and she was the vessel through which it would be created and sustained.

She lived on crazy faith.

As the school continued to grow, Mary realized that she needed bigger facilities. She had been watching for *the* spot where she should next go, including a field called "Hell's Hole," which was being used as a dump. She prayed and came to believe that God was telling her that this parcel of land was where she should next go. She approached the landowner, determined to buy the property. The price was $250. Mary began to broker a deal and finally got the man to sell it to her for $5 down with the balance to be paid in two years. Mary said, "I promised to be back in a few days with the initial payment. He never knew it, but I didn't have five dollars. I raised the sum selling ice cream and sweet-potato pies to workmen on construction jobs, and I took the owner his money in small change wrapped in my handkerchief."[16]

Mary's business acumen drew the attention of wealthy businessmen. Shortly after her purchase of Hell's Hole, industrialist James Gamble approached her and wanted to know more about what she was doing. She gave him a tour of the land that she had just purchased and told him her plans. He was so impressed that he and some other businessmen decided to help her; eventually, they became her board of trustees.[17]

Mary continued to come in contact with people who were interested in helping her build her school, which was always improving and expanding. In 1923, her Daytona Institute merged with Cookman Institute, which had been a school for African American boys, becoming Bethune-Cookman College.

Mary was seeing, and would later give testament to, the fact that crazy faith really does work.

Mary's life is filled with stories of how she kept on believing in the power and presence of God. So many of her circumstances and predicaments were scary, and so much of what God told her to do seemed impossible and even stupid, yet God came through every time.

Mary McLeod Bethune went from being a poor, uneducated "colored" girl to an internationally known educator, scholar, and businesswoman who happened to be an African American. No obstacle ever stopped her. Once the scales fell from her eyes on her first day of school, she was like a bird that had been pushed from its nest. She went from not knowing she had wings to understanding that her wings worked and could take flight. She was like that ant—she had "high hopes" and crazy, crazy faith.

Crazy-Faith Challenge

Crazy faith makes us do more than *believe* that God has something for us to do; it moves us to the certainty of *knowing* what God wants us to do. It was Mary McLeod Bethune's knowledge that gave her an almost superhuman energy to accompany her knowledge of God's plans for her life, and that knowledge never stopped fueling her. Do you feel knowledge like that? If not, is it something that you think you want to feel? And where is God leading you?

conclusion
the miracles around us

The psalmist wrote, "When I consider your heavens, the work of your fingers, the moon and the stars, which you have set in place, what is man that you are mindful of him, and the son of man, that you care for him?" (Psalm 8:3-4). The psalmist stopped to absorb the greatness of God, and what he sees astounds him: "O LORD, our Lord, how majestic is your name in all the earth!" (Psalm 8:1). Looking around, he sees all that God has set in place, and it occurs to him that it is crazy *not* to think that nothing is too hard or impossible for God.

Having faith and especially this thing called "crazy faith," believing that nothing is impossible for God, takes time to develop. There is a spiritual strengthening process that we must go through to get mature faith. That is crazy faith. And our spiritual strengthening pits us directly against the way we are taught to survive and thrive in the world, which is to ask questions and try to make the things for which we strive seem pragmatic and logical. Faith works directly against that worldly model, and for that reason we really struggle. We grow up learning to fear—fear rejection, fear failure, fear success—and we learn those lessons well. Those fears drive us to limit what we can do and ultimately what God can do.

It is not hard, then, to understand why getting any level of faith is difficult. It's like learning a song incorrectly and then trying to learn it the right way. It takes forever to make the corrections in one's spirit and mind. It takes a long time to get rid of the ideas that have been ingrained in us. For example, if you had always been told that you are stupid and then one day someone told you that you're brilliant, it would take a long time to start believing a new truth. Or, if you once were overweight and then lost weight, it would take a while to see and accept yourself differently. We live with our pasts—past ideas, past lessons, and past experiences. Far too often those "pasts" get in the way of our moving forward.

Fear is a formidable obstacle to having faith. Fear cancels faith, and that is a problem because the Bible clearly says, "Without faith it is impossible to please God" (Hebrews 11:6). It is the struggle between living "in the spirit" and "living in the flesh." Most of us live in the flesh. It is how we are trained to live. People with great confidence, as opposed to having great faith, live in the flesh, living to please themselves and not God. When we decide that we want to please God, we are giving God and our spirits a necessary shift, for us to find a way to live above our fears or get God to get rid of our fears. Fear is replaced with faith in an entity whom we cannot see or touch and many times, especially before we grow spiritually, cannot hear.

That's a big assignment. It's all part of the process, but it is a huge assignment nonetheless.

The Bible explains how living in the flesh is antithetical to living in the Spirit. In Romans, Paul writes, "Those who live according to the sinful nature have their minds set on what nature desires; but those who live in accordance with the Spirit have their minds set on what the Spirit desires....The sinful mind is hostile to God. It does not submit to God's law, nor can it do so. Those controlled by the sinful nature cannot please God" (Romans 8:5-8). Later on, Paul assures all believers, "You did not receive a spirit that makes you a slave again to fear, but you received the Spirit of sonship" (Romans 8:15). If sin is defined as anything that separates us from God, then fear is understood to be a sin because it gets in the way of trusting and believing in God from the bottoms of our souls. Fear reins us in by telling us that our faith in God is stupid, and we reject a faith that really does seem stupid.

And by human standards, crazy faith is stupid. When we study Paul, the ex-murderer who became perhaps the greatest of all preachers and teachers for Jesus, we marvel at his vision—a world filled with people, Jews and Gentiles, who accept Jesus and live according to Jesus' teachings. Paul's crazy faith made him go into places where he knew he would be ambushed; it made him teach masses of people in the face of hostile government officials. It made him dare to listen to the voice of God, even as a prisoner, and instruct his captors on what they should do. It made him, on the voyage that ended in shipwreck, deliver a mini-sermon to his captors, not knowing what their reaction would be. The ship was wrecked, the voyagers had no food for days, and Paul was still a prisoner. But Paul's crazy faith made him say to them, "You should have taken my advice not to sail from Crete....But now I urge you to keep up your courage, because not one of you will be lost; only the ship will be destroyed. Last night an angel of the God whose I am and whom I serve stood beside me and said, 'Do not be afraid, Paul. You must stand trial before Caesar; and God has graciously given you the lives of all who sail with you.' So keep up your courage, men, for I have faith in God that it will happen just as he told me" (Acts 27:21-25).

This speech wasn't logical. It couldn't have been easy for Paul to tell to a group of burly men who had his life in their hands that he had just been talked to by an angel. But by that time, Paul had developed a crazy faith that said no matter what happened, it would be all right. Better than that, it would be just as God said it would be.

Paul's journey to having crazy faith was helped along by his experience on the road to Damascus. To hear the Lord's voice, be struck blind, and then receive sight again after three days, as Paul did, would be enough to move anyone from fear to faith. In fact, such experiences would make one afraid *not* to believe. Paul's journey, though, had already started. There had to have been an opening in Paul's spirit into which God could enter.

That "opening" is what God looks for in us, and the more we want to believe in God totally, the bigger the opening becomes, allowing more and more of God's Spirit to pervade our humanness.

But how does the opening get there? How does a growing faith get its beginning? As I said at the very beginning of this book, we're talking about three levels of faith: mere faith, real faith, and, finally, crazy faith.

Mere faith is that which we get by virtue of being in church or being around people who talk about God. When we are babes in the flesh and in the spirit, we don't understand what people are saying when they say, "God can do everything but fail." We just know that we hear people talking about God. We are taught to say our evening prayers. In my family, we were taught that God was everywhere. "Don't you think you can act up and God not know it," my mother would tell me. "God sees everything you do!" That pronouncement weighed heavily on me. I believed it. Whenever I did something wrong, I would immediately look up to see if I could see God looking at me.

Wangari Maathai, a Kenyan woman who was the first woman in East Africa to earn a PhD and the first African woman to win a Nobel Peace Prize, lives by crazy faith. In her country, trees were being destroyed in vast numbers. The forests in Kenya had shrunk to less than 5 percent of what they had been originally. There were many consequences of this, not least of which was that women, who had to gather wood in order to do their work, had to travel farther and farther to get what they needed. Maathai was bothered both by the deforestation and by the fact that the women were losing valuable time with their children as they traveled great distances to get wood. Something had to be done. Maathai says that she heard a voice that said, "Plant trees." That was God. God not only said to plant trees but also told her how many to plant: seven. And so she did.

As she began, she was ridiculed. The men told her that she was out of line, that no woman had ever planted a tree before, and so it was impossible. But Maathai, who today still talks about the need to listen to God, listened to God at that point, and since she didn't hear the Lord tell her not to plant trees, she went ahead and planted seven trees in her backyard. Other women saw her and began to do the same. If they asked her how to plant the trees, she would say, "Do what you know." And they did. The result was that her crazy faith resulted in literally millions of trees being planted all over Kenya. There are now thirty million more trees in Kenya than there were when she began her project, all of them planted by untrained Kenyan women.

There is yet another story that might help bring about understanding of what crazy faith is. There was a woman in my congregation who suffered from serious liver disease. She had two transplants and was waiting for a third, and it seemed that no compatible liver could be found for her. She was very sick. I began praying for her, *demanding* that God give her a new liver and a new life. I was praying in "real faith" mode. I knew that God was real and that God could do anything. But my adolescent spirit (I was not an adolescent, but my spirit was still there) made me pray like a spoiled teenager, pouting because God didn't do my bidding. I questioned God, but I was not about to leave God. My faith by then was too strong. I knew that God could do anything; I was confused about why the Lord would not heal this woman.

I had an all-night prayer vigil at my home, praying not so much for this woman, but for an answer from God. I was wrestling with

God, like Jacob did (Genesis 32:24). I was not about to let go until God blessed me with an answer. What I wanted was *my* answer, not God's, but I didn't realize that until late into the wee hours of the morning.

I wept, I cried, I railed against God. What good was prayer, I wondered, if you are not going to answer? Finally, at about five o'clock in the morning, I heard God's voice: "You have not been praying the right thing."

Of course, that made me angry. I *was* praying the right thing. I was praying for God to heal this woman and for God to answer me! I was indignant, but that voice said, "You have been praying for your will to be done. You must pray for my will to be done."

Well, that wasn't acceptable either, because in my heart I felt like God's will was that this woman should die. I said as much to God. Then I realized how that must have sounded. There was no other "voice" from God, only silence, and as I realized what God had said to me, I crumpled and cried even more.

"Okay," I said between my sobs, "let your will be done. Let your will be done. But if it is your will, please give me peace about it and give her family peace too."

When I went to the hospital later that day, I was surprised. I *was* at peace. The woman was still very sick; jaundice had set in, and she was as yellow as a traffic "yield" sign. But I leaned down and sang into her ear, and I realized if she was going to die, I wanted to leave her with a sense of my peace as well. Her family was there, and they too seemed to be at peace.

And then out of nowhere, a liver was found for this woman, and today she is alive. There was no logical reason, no warning, no hint that a liver would be found. The donor banks had all but given up. And then the miracle happened. I realized, though, that a miracle had happened with me even before the liver was found: my level of trust deepened in a way that could not be shaken.

Whatever God was going to do was all right, and I knew I would be all right. It was a life-changing moment.

That incident was one of several that moved me from having real faith to having crazy faith. That someone could be moments away from death and then be given life did something to my understanding and appreciation for who God is and what God can do. In this growing phase of my spiritual life, I learned that when we trust God totally, when we can say, "Be it done to me as you have said," God equips us to handle whatever is about to happen; and when we have crazy faith, we know that to be true, beyond a doubt.

God doesn't expect us to get from mere faith to crazy faith without some help, and that's why God graces us with miracles. We don't often see them or pay attention to them, but they are there.

One of the greatest miracles just happened to you: you just took a breath. That happened because God, in his amazing creative genius, created lungs and a diaphragm with a mechanism that only God could have devised. Your heart just beat several times, making it possible for blood to flow throughout your body and keep you alive. Those are miracles, things that don't have to be, things that defy logic and human capability, but they just are.

When we become aware of the miracles around us, the journey from mere faith to crazy faith becomes easier. We can actually *see the greatness of God* and begin to understand that since God did all of this, there really is nothing that God cannot do. Finding a way to *see* God feeds us in ways that we cannot begin to imagine.

Bill Hybels, the senior pastor of Willow Creek Community Church in Illinois, wrote a book called *Too Busy Not to Pray*, and in that book he gives a formula for praying that is very helpful in getting people to see God. He uses an acronym, ACTS, which stands for "adoration, confession, thanksgiving, supplication." What happens when you pray using that formula, in the "adoration" phase, is that you see God in creation. You see things that you never noticed before, and you begin to understand how great God is. Adoring God is different from thanking God. We thank God for what he does for us, but we adore God for being God. God places miracles around us, and when we adore him, we see those miracles, or at least we begin to think about them. We begin to see the connections between what we have always been surrounded by and what we never took time to credit God for. It is like Alice Walker says in *The Color Purple:* How can one see the color purple and not be amazed?[1] In fact, how can we look at any of the colors that we see daily and not be amazed? How does a little seed go into the ground and grow to be a brilliant flower or plant? High hopes—faith?

There are so many miracles around us. We didn't create them, God did, and the benefit of taking note of them is that they reassure us of God's omnipotence. No matter how "great" we are, we will never be as great as God. That thought should give us confidence and the energy needed to beat back our fears and place ourselves in the hands of God completely, so that we can say, "Be it done unto me according to your will." We have to remember the woman with the jars of oil, the bridge builder, the educator, Gideon and his army, the unnamed woman who believed that she would be healed. They represent, and lived lives to, the glory of God because they believed in God's power to act on their behalf. They are miracles.

And the miracles around us help us move from mere faith to crazy faith, and they remind us that with such a Creator as this on our side, there really isn't anything that we cannot do, because there isn't anything that God cannot do. Believing this means that you have, absolutely and positively, embraced crazy faith.

notes

ⓔ ⓔ ⓔ

Chapter 2: Before I Be a Slave

1. Anthony Sampson, *Mandela: The Authorized Biography* (New York: Vintage Books, 2000), 328.
2. Ibid., 66.
3. Ibid., 7–9.
4. Ibid., 78–79.
5. Ibid., 62.
6. Ibid.
7. Ibid., 63.
8. Ibid., 67–68.
9. Nelson Mandela, *Long Walk to Freedom: The Autobiography of Nelson Mandela* (Boston: Little Brown, 1994), 162.
10. Ibid.
11. Ibid.
12. Ibid., 174.
13. Ibid., 174–75.
14. Ibid., 200.
15. Ibid., 237.
16. Ibid., 238.
17. Ibid.
18. Ibid., 259.
19. Ibid.
20. Ibid., 267.

21. Ibid., 317.
22. Ibid., 350.
23. Ibid., 375–76.
24. Sampson, *Mandela*, 230.
25. Ibid., 203.
26. Ibid., 204.
27. Ibid.
28. Ibid., 212.
29. Ibid.
30. Ibid., 392.
31. Ibid., 396.

ⓔ ⓔ ⓔ

Chapter 4: Roses and a Key
1. Chris Gardner, with Quincy Troupe and Mim Eichler Rivas, *The Pursuit of Happyness* (New York: Amistad, 2006), 8.
2. Ibid., 9.
3. Ibid.
4. Ibid.
5. Ibid., 6.
6. Ibid., 235.
7. Ibid., 239.
8. Ibid., 241.
9. Ibid., 249.
10. Ibid.
11. Ibid., 258.
12. Ibid., 300.

ⓔ ⓔ ⓔ

Chapter 6: Waiting for Deliverance
1. Catherine Clinton, *Harriet Tubman: The Road to Freedom* (New York: Little, Brown, 2004), 85.

2. Ibid.

3. Jean McMahon Humez, *Harriet Tubman: The Life and the Life Stories* (Madison: University of Wisconsin Press, 2003), 211–12.

4. Ibid., 212.

5. Ibid., 177.

6. Kate Clifford Larson, *Bound for the Promised Land: Harriet Tubman; Portrait of an American Hero* (New York: Ballantine Books, 2004), 42.

7. Ibid., 43.

8. Clinton, *Harriet Tubman*, 91.

9. Ibid.

10. Ibid., 83.

11. Humez, *Harriet Tubman*, 217.

12. Ibid., 232.

13. Ibid.

14. Ibid.

15. Ibid.

ⓔ ⓔ ⓔ

Chapter 8: Where to Go, Not How to Get There

1. José Luis González-Balado, *Mother Teresa: Her Life, Her Work, Her Message; A Memoir* (Liguori, MO: Liguori Publications, 1997), 46.

2. Navin Chawla, *Mother Teresa* (Rockport, MA: Element Books, 1996), 7.

3. Ibid., 8.

4. González-Balado, *Mother Teresa*, 58.

5. Ibid., 60.

6. Kathryn Spink, *Mother Teresa: A Complete Authorized Biography* (San Francisco: HarperSanFrancisco, 1997), 23–24.

7. Ibid., 57.

8. Ibid., 80.

9. Ibid., 68.

10. González-Balado, *Mother Teresa*, 68.

11. Ibid.

12. Ibid.

13. Spink, *Mother Teresa*, 69.

14. Ibid., 93.

15. Ibid., 80.

16. Ibid., 159.

17. Chawla, *Mother Teresa*, xvi.

ⓔ ⓔ ⓔ

Chapter 9: The Most Audacious Touch

1. The Information on customs that follows here is taken from Elizabeth Fletcher, "Major Events in a Woman's Life" (http://www.womeninthebible.net/3.2.Major_Events.htm).

ⓔ ⓔ ⓔ

Chapter 10: The Eighth Wonder of the World

1. David McCullough, *The Great Bridge: The Epic Story of the Building of the Brooklyn Bridge* (New York: Simon & and Shuster, 1972), 41.

2. Elizabeth Mann, *The Brooklyn Bridge* (New York: Mikaya Press, 1996), 5.

3. McCullough, *The Great Bridge*, 28.

4. Ibid., 29.

5. Ibid., 30.

6. Ibid., 31.

7. Ibid., 73.

8. Ibid., 93.

9. Ibid., 454.

10. Ibid.

11. Ibid.

12. Ibid., 318.

13. Ibid., 321.
14. Ibid.
15. Ibid., 463.
16. Ibid.
17. Ibid., 516.
18. Ibid., 517.

☉ ☉ ☉
Chapter 11: How Shall They Eat?
1. See William Barclay, *The Gospel of Matthew*, vol. 2 (Louisville: Westminster John Knox, 2001), 119–21.
2. Muhammad Yunus, "Poverty Is a Threat to Peace," Nobel Peace Prize Lecture, December 10, 2006 (http://nobelprize.org/nobel_prizes/peace/laureates/2006/yunus-lecture-en.html).
3. Ibid.
4. Ibid.
5. Ibid.

☉ ☉ ☉
Chapter 12: The Scales Fell from My Eyes
1. "High Hopes," music by Jimmy Van Heusen, lyrics by Sammy Cahn.
2. Charles Spurgeon Johnson, interview with Mary McLeod Bethune (http://www.floridamemory.com/onlineClassroom/MaryBethune/interview.cfm), 1.
3. Ibid.
4. Ibid.
5. Ibid.
6. Ibid.
7. Bernice Anderson Poole, *Mary McLeod Bethune: Educator* (Los Angeles: Holloway House, 1994), 78.

8. Johnson, interview with Mary McLeod Bethune, 1.

9. Ibid.

10. Ibid.

11. R. Brian Wright, "The Idealistic Realist: Mary McLeod Bethune, The National Council of Negro Women and The National Youth Administration" (MA thesis, Virginia Polytechnic Institute and State University, 1999), 6 (available online: http://scholar.lib.vt.edu/theses/available/etd-050799-140251/unrestricted/thesis3.pdf).

12. Ibid., 7.

13. Ibid.

14. Ibid.

15. Ibid.

16. Ibid., 8.

17. Ibid.

ⓔ ⓔ ⓔ

Conclusion: The Miracles around Us

1. Alice Walker, *The Color Purple* (New York: Washington Square Press, 1983).